ENCIRCLED·BY Love

ENCIRCLED·BY Love

JILL C. MAJOR
LAUREN C. LEIFSON
HOLLIE C. BEVAN

Deseret Book Company
Salt Lake City, Utah

Quotations from the *Ensign* on pp. 26-27, 46-47, 48, and 87, copyright
©1973, 1980, 1981, and 1985 by The Church of Jesus Christ of Latter-day
Saints. Reprinted with permission.

Library of Congress Catalog Card No. 89-51133
ISBN 0-87579-247-2

Printed in the United States of America
10   9   8   7   6   5   4   3   2   1

To my eternal companion, Kenneth A. Major. As a young elder he encircled me with love and patiently led me back to the Church. Through the example of his constant concern, care, and love for me and our children, I have learned to love others.

—Jill C. Major

To my best friend, Bret, and to all of those family members, friends, and strangers who have encircled me with love.

—Lauren C. Leifson

To Him who has ransomed my soul that I might follow Him in loving others. I have truly been encircled in the arms of His love.

—Hollie C. Bevan

Contents

Preface

Encircled By Love was written to help motivate you to do the work necessary to obtain and maintain loving relationships. We hope this book will increase your knowledge of how to effectively communicate love, and will help you gain the courage to overcome fears so that you can partake of the fruits of love more freely.

The title of our book, *Encircled By Love*, is taken from the scriptures. Lehi, when he was very close to death, exclaimed, "But behold, the Lord hath redeemed my soul from hell; I have beheld his glory, and I am encircled about eternally in the arms of his love." (2 Nephi 1:15.) In the Doctrine and Covenants the Lord told Oliver Cowdery, "Be faithful and diligent in keeping the commandments of God, and I will encircle thee in the arms of my love." (D&C 6:20.) We know from the scriptures that God's love "sheddeth itself abroad in the hearts of the children of men; wherefore, it is the most desirable above all things." (1 Nephi 11:22.) Truly, there is still love to be found on the earth. It radiates forth from our Heavenly Father and our brother, Jesus Christ, and it is found in the hearts of many of our spiritual siblings whom we now call neighbors, friends, family, and even strangers. It is found in your heart!

Women, especially, have a great endowment of charity, which is surely an inheritance that comes from our Heavenly Mother as well as our Heavenly Father. We are the ones chosen to nurture and nourish our Heavenly Father's children when they are sent to the earth. These God-given feelings create a strong bond of love between sisters in the gospel. We need each other!

Jill Major discovered the important roles women can play in the lives of each other. Her sister-in-law and close friend, Janet, was dying of cancer, and Jill felt deeply the pain she was going through.

"My husband, Ken, was always by my side, and yet I felt that I needed more—another woman, a sister, to help strengthen me while I helped strengthen Janet," Jill says. Impressed with the loving nature of Lauren Leifson, a woman who had recently moved into her ward, Jill reached out to Lauren for additional love and support.

Janet's death threw Jill into a deep depression. Overwhelmed with feelings of guilt and loss, she gradually shut herself off from all expressions of love. Jill continues her story:

> One night I lay in the darkness of my bedroom and sobbed, "I cannot take any more." I no longer wanted to exist. I was not suicidal—I wasn't thinking about taking my own life. I just didn't want to be part of life anymore. My husband held me close, rocking me like an infant. When I calmed down Ken put his hands on my head and gave me a priesthood blessing. "You will be able to get help," he promised me.
>
> God has always answered my prayers. I had faith that I would be able to get help, but I assumed the help would come from a hospital or a clinic. I have since learned that God often answers prayers through those who are closest to you. The next day my friend, Donna, called long distance from California. She tried to shake me out of the blackness. "I want to help you. I love you," she said over and over again. The words slipped off me and fell as if I were wearing a love-proof slicker. In desperation she called Lauren. "Talk to Jill. She needs our help."

Late the next evening the phone rang. "Hi, there," Lauren chirped cheerfully. "Let's talk."

"Okay," I said, feeling it was anything but okay. "What do you want to talk about?" She skillfully guided the conversation to my depression.

"How do you know I am depressed?" I challenged her.

Lauren replied, "Jill, some of the light is gone."

"I don't want to talk about this," I snapped.

She was undaunted. "Jill, I want to share this burden you are carrying. Please talk to me."

I recoiled. My heart started pounding. "No! I cannot share this burden. It is too heavy. I am all alone with this one. No one can help me."

Lauren is the type of person who would never intrude on someone's privacy, but this time she would not back off.

"Jill, there is a scripture that says we are to share each other's burdens. You need to share so your friends can help you carry this load."

A dim light of hope flickered in the distance. *Perhaps she is right,* I thought.

I began telling Lauren all that had happened in the preceding months—about the little hurts that had become so deep and painful that at times I wondered if I would ever stop hurting again. The conversation went on for hours. Finally I was talked out. Exhausted, I whispered, "Thank you for calling me. I feel better."

"You're welcome," she said. "We will talk again soon. Jill?"

"What?" I answered.

"I love you." Those words echoed down to the depths of my heart and I felt love for the first time in weeks. Not only did I feel Lauren's love, but I also felt the love of many other friends and family members who had shown such great concern during this trial.

When you learn to love others with Christlike compassion, the bonds of charity will enwrap your soul with a sweet peace that cannot justly be described with words. You will have a sure knowledge of the love that our Heavenly Father has for you. Having once felt that love, you will naturally want others to feel it also. It will not matter if those people are friends or strangers, because you will recognize them and know them as your brothers and sisters. This sure knowledge will aid you in encircling others with love.

Hollie Bevan tells of an experience she and her husband had in extending life-saving love to a stranger:

> One day, as my husband and I were traveling home on the freeway, I felt prompted to turn and look back. To my horror, I saw someone ready to jump from the freeway overpass.
>
> My husband slammed the brakes to the floor and shoved the car into reverse. Within seconds, we were racing backwards. "Don't worry," he assured me, "it's probably just a kid playing on the bridge."
>
> My husband stepped out of his side of the car and yelled, "Hey! You weren't thinking of jumping, were you?" Then he lowered his head through the open window, and I could see that his face had paled to a chalk white. "It's a man," he uttered in apparent shock, "and he's crying."
>
> I quickly hopped up onto the trunk and yelled, "What's your name?" The man yelled back this in-formation and I told him our names. I continued yelling questions as I mentally noted his position on the bridge. He was sitting on the very edge, his bare feet dangling. His hands were positioned at the point of support that barely kept him from slipping to the concrete below and his head was lowered, as if from the weight of an enormous burden.

Boldly, I asked, "What happened today to make you want to kill yourself?" Through sobs, he told us of his deep despair. By this time, others had also stopped on the freeway to try to help. As they tried to come close to him, he would inch forward, threatening to jump if they continued pressing his space. Even so, he kept responding to us, answering the questions that I kept asking. Sensing his trust, we told him that my husband would remain on the freeway below to talk to him and that he should keep his focus on me and watch me drive the car to the next overpass and on to the frontage road that looped up to the bridge, where he clung to an ounce of hope. He agreed.

I stopped the car about six feet from where he was positioned and slowly stepped forward, all the while telling the man to listen only to my voice. "I'm walking toward you now. I'm six feet from you and stepping to your right." His eyes remained fixed on the concrete below, but he responded, "Okay."

Finally, I grabbed the young man's elbow and he allowed me to help him back over the side to safety. Then I escorted him to the back seat of our car. As soon as it was apparent that the young man was safely seated, a gentleman in a business suit rushed up to the young man's side and threw his arms around him. Tears were streaming down this onlooker's face as he sobbed, "I don't know you, but I love you. Please live! Please, I care." He wiped his tears with his tie and gave the down-hearted man another hug; then he pressed some money into the young man's hand and departed.

Because of her great love, Hollie reached out and pulled a young man off a bridge. The onlooker, surely a brother, literally encircled a stranger in the arms of his love. Together they saved a mortal life. As you develop charity you can also reach out, encircling others with the love of Christ. Perhaps, in doing so, you will help save a spiritual life.

CHAPTER 1

Encircle Thyself with Love

Often the commandment "Thou shalt love thy neighbor as thyself" (D&C 59:6) is divided in two parts: some people put the
emphasis on loving their neighbors and others on loving themselves. But this scripture was given as a whole, for we cannot
truly love ourselves without loving our neighbors, nor can we
truly love our neighbors without loving ourselves. We are in-
separably linked to each other as brothers and sisters.

Paul counseled Timothy, whom he called "my own son in
the faith" (1 Timothy 1:2): "Neglect not the gift that is in
thee. . . . Take heed unto thyself, and unto the doctrine; continue in them: for in doing this thou shalt both save thyself, and
them that hear thee" (1 Timothy 4:14, 16). Each time you
develop a talent, seek a spiritual gift, learn a new principle of
the gospel, overcome a weakness, or conquer a fault, you not
only benefit yourself, but you also become a better neighbor. You
can give more because there is more of you to give.

The Lord has commanded, "When thou art converted,
strengthen thy brethren." (Luke 22:32.) As you love your neighbor, you will strengthen her, and she in turn will become a better
neighbor and be able to strengthen you. This, then, becomes an
eternal circle, where to give love to your neighbor is to love
yourself and to love yourself is to give love to your neighbor.

One sister learned firsthand of this cycle of love through the
following experience:

A new neighbor moved in down the street. Again and again, I thought, "I should go over and meet her," but I didn't. When she didn't appear at church, I concluded that she was either inactive or a nonmember. Later, I learned that she was facing the challenge of single parenthood. Once my neighbor was out working in her garden and I stopped by and introduced myself. Those few words were our only contact for a year and a half.

Then in April, as I listened to the general conference talks, I once again thought of my neighbor. Immediately I went to the telephone. "Hello," I said somewhat timidly. "I am your neighbor two houses down. I am looking for a walking partner and was wondering if you like to walk."

My neighbor said that she would rather ride her bike, but that she would give walking a try, so we set up a biweekly walking date. Each step we took together I learned more about my neighbor's needs. I learned how difficult it is to be a single mother, and how frustrating, at times, to be a non-Mormon in a Mormon community. My neighbor also learned about my needs. During that time my little two-year-old niece was dying of cancer. Many times my neighbor offered comfort. "I will pray for you and for her," she told me.

Then came the call that we had been expecting for a long time. "Deborah died last night," my mother said quietly. I went for a long walk that morning, crying out within my heart to Heavenly Father, pleading with him to comfort my sister, whose arms were so empty at that moment. When I returned, my neighbor came to my door. "I heard," was all she said. Then she enfolded me in her arms and I wept.

I reached out to my neighbor, and in my trial,

my Heavenly Father sent my neighbor to strengthen
me and give me comfort.

It is of paramount importance that we learn to care for ourselves so that we can more fully care for others. Temporally or
spiritually, we cannot feed the hungry if our table is empty. We
cannot offer water from an empty well to one who is thirsty. We
cannot take in a stranger if we have no roof over our head. Nor
can we clothe the naked, feed the sick, or visit those in prison,
if we ourselves are without clothes, unable to lift our heads from
bed, or caged behind prison bars. In order for us to spread hap-
piness to others, we first must be of good cheer. To be able to
bear our testimonies, we must first build our own testimonies.
To fulfill the commandment to love others completely, we must
first love ourselves completely.

Do we love ourselves as well as we love our neighbors? Do
we treat ourselves with kindness, gentleness, and tenderness? We
should, but many of us don't. Neal A. Maxwell observed, "Some
of us who would not chastise a neighbor for his frailties have a
field day with our own. Some of us stand before no more harsh
a judge than ourselves, a judge who stubbornly refuses to admit
much happy evidence and who cares nothing for due process."
In the morning we go to the mirror, take one look at ourselves,
and say, "Yuck! You look awful. Boy, are you getting old. Look
at those wrinkles and crow's feet. You shouldn't have had that
dish of ice cream last night. You're putting on weight." Now,
would you offer such criticisms to your friend? Or even your
enemy? When you make a mistake, are you forgiving, or does
your mind scream, "Boy, that was stupid. How can you be so
dumb?" Then do you continue to deride yourself for days without
any mercy? Can you imagine saying to a friend, "You don't have
any talents. You're not good at anything"? Of course not, but
many of us whisper those dreadful things in our own minds.

If any of this sounds familiar to you, try practicing these two
precious additions to the golden rule.

The golden rule: Do unto others as you would have them do
unto you.

The silver rule: Do unto *yourself* as you would have others do unto you.

The bronze rule: Love yourself as your Heavenly Father loves you.

Let's begin with the silver rule. Consider how you would want your best and dearest friend to treat you. Would you want that person to be critical, judgmental, harsh, or unkind? Of course not. Every person on the earth has faults; no one likes to have them pointed out. Moroni struggled with his weakness in writing and feared that the Gentiles would mock his words, but Christ said unto him, "I give unto men weakness that they may be humble; and my grace is sufficient for all men that humble themselves before me; for if they humble themselves before me, and have faith in me, then will I make weak things become strong unto them. . . . And . . . Moroni, having heard these words, was comforted." (Ether 12:27, 29.)

One man of our acquaintance truly symbolizes the ideal of loving yourself. On Christmas morning, as everyone is hurriedly tearing paper and "oohing" over gifts, he waits patiently. After everyone else's gifts are opened there is always one gift left under the tree. He silently walks over to the Christmas tree, reaches down, and picks up the gift. The tag reads: To Bill, From Bill. Isn't that great? Every year he goes out and buys himself a present. Every year he gets just what he wants. What a terrific tradition!

Be your own best friend rather than your own worst critic. Start by giving yourself daily emotional and mental boosters. Lock yourself in the bathroom, face the mirror, and say a minimum of one nice thing about yourself to yourself every morning or evening. If you can think of ten or twenty nice things about yourself, say them. Many people, however, have an extremely difficult time thinking of, let alone saying, even one thing nice about themselves. They get confused because they don't understand the difference between bragging and boosting. Bragging is simply giving yourself boosters in public; it is not a good substitute for daily private boosters. Christ taught that those who "sound a trumpet" before them "that they may have glory of men" already

4

have their reward. (Matthew 6:2.) Bragging increases self-centeredness. Daily boosters, however, if done honestly and privately, can build self-esteem and self-worth.

So take a good look at yourself in the mirror. Examine yourself physically. Do you have beautiful skin, pretty hands, straight white teeth, or attractive hair? Try saying out loud, "I have beautiful eyes," or if you can't quite say those words then say, "Heavenly Father really gave me beautiful eyes."

Next, examine your emotional self. Did you control your temper today? Did you express love, concern, or compassion to anyone around you?

Now, look at your spiritual self. Do you feel close to Heavenly Father? Did you lovingly serve any of his children, which includes your family, neighbors, friends, or business associates? Did you read your scriptures, attend a church meeting, take the sacrament worthily?

After just a few minutes of asking yourself these questions, you should have a mental list of several positive attributes. Choose one and say it out loud while looking in the mirror. No booster is insignificant, no matter how small it may appear to you, and it will help you think of yourself more positively, more lovingly.

Next let's consider the bronze rule: Love yourself as your Heavenly Father loves you. The veil, which was placed over us at birth, was necessary in order for us to be tested. We don't remember exactly what happened in our premortal existence, but we do know that we lived with our heavenly parents and brothers and sisters. We lived as a family—exactly the way this earth life was designed. Parallels can be drawn between our heavenly family and our earthly family.

Consider an eleven-month-old child who is just learning how to walk. The mother and father place him tenderly on the floor, steady his arms and legs, and then back away to the other side of the room. The little child gets concerned when left to his own abilities and begins whimpering for help. The mother and father speak softly to him, quieting him and encouraging him to take one little step. The child's knees begin to tremble; his face now is pleading for assistance. Mother says, "Come on, sweetheart.

I know you can do it. Just take one little step." The toddler studies the faces of his parents, looking for the faith in him that he lacks in himself. Then he takes courage and inches one tiny foot forward. Mother and Father are thrilled and applaud his wonderful accomplishment. "You see, honey. You can do it," Father says. "Now take another step. You are getting closer to us all the time." After many days of practice the toddler finally makes it all the way across the room and falls into the open arms of his parents. "I knew you could do it. I am so proud of you," the father says joyfully. There is delight in the child's bright eyes. He grins as he realizes his accomplishment and feels the joy radiating from his parents.

This example parallels the way our Heavenly Father deals with us. He places us down on earth, but to him, it is no more than just across the room, for he is always near. Then he holds his arms out to us, saying, "Little child, I have faith in you. You can succeed. I gave you the talents and capabilities required to fulfill your special mission. I am with you and you are near me. Continue in your course. You will get closer to me all the time. Just keep trying." With courage gained from the Lord's counsel, we experience great joy and delight within ourselves as we take each tiny step along life's path. Then one day we will fall into the loving arms of our Heavenly Father and hear, "I knew you could do it. I am so proud of you!" or, in the Savior's words, "Well done, thou good and faithful servant . . . enter thou into the joy of thy lord." (Matthew 25:21.) But such success takes practice; we must strive for it every day. If we fall down, our Heavenly Father walks back across the room, just as any loving parent would do, helps us up (if we will allow him to), steadies us, and then encourages us to try again. Over and over again this scene takes place.

Sometimes we fail to recognize this divine assistance because our Heavenly Father uses other mortals to lift us up. Jill relates how our Heavenly Father came to her aid in a time of need:

Several years ago, I prayed that Heavenly Father would bless our home with a baby girl. In due time, he blessed us with not one, but two daughters. Twins! When we brought our two little angels home from the hospital, I thought it would be the beginning of the greatest, happiest life ever, but it wasn't. *It was horrible!* The Lord had obviously multiplied our joys and our sorrows. Both Pamela and Patricia had colic and they screamed twelve hours a day. The nights brought some relief, although the babies took turns waking up, so both my husband, Ken, and I were often up three or four times each. Many people came to help, but as the weeks went by, we grew more tired and despondent.

In church one Sunday, Ken and I each had several turns taking crying babies out in the hall. The words to the closing song began, "There is an hour of peace and rest . . . " Ken tilted his head and whispered in my ear, "Not at our house." Funny? It wasn't then, and I immediately started to cry. To hide my embarrassment I escaped out of the church during the prayer and walked home.

Days and nights became a blur of baths, bottles, diapers, and the ever-commanding bawling in stereo. Finally, I just didn't feel like I could cope one more day. Mentally, physically, and emotionally exhausted, I fell to my knees. "Heavenly Father, please send me some help!" I pleaded.

A few evenings later I was trying to escape the turmoil by walking around our subdivision.

It was dark when I trudged past Jackie's house. "Jill, is that you?" Jackie called out.

"Yes," I said from across the street.

"Are you alone?"

"Yes."

"Would you like some company?" Jackie asked.

I was so drained that I really didn't want to talk with anyone, yet good manners kept me from being honest. "Sure," I said, "that would be great."

As we walked through the night I began to tell Jackie all that was really going on in my home, and as we talked, I felt my burdens ease and I didn't feel quite so frazzled.

It was half an hour before Jackie said, "Jill, are you getting tired yet?" Not until then did I realize that Jackie was not out there for exercise: she was out there to keep me from getting mugged in the dark; she was out there because she had a feeling that she was needed; she was out there, sent by Heavenly Father, as an answer to my desperate prayer.

With infinite patience and love our heavenly parents lift us and encourage us. Should we not be as patient, loving, understanding, and compassionate with ourselves?

"Thou shalt love thy neighbor as *thyself*." We must keep the whole commandment and not divide it into parts. We should continue to live the golden rule, but add to that the other precious rules. You are a child of heavenly parents. You are of infinite worth, so remember to do unto yourself as you would have others do unto you and love yourself as your Heavenly Father loves you.

CHAPTER 2

Love Encircles Through Service

Jesus said that the first and great commandment is, "Thou shalt love the Lord thy God with all thy heart, and with all thy soul, and with all thy mind." Then he continued, "The second is *like unto* it, Thou shalt love thy neighbour as thyself." (Matthew 22:37-39; italics added.) Indeed, the second commandment is a measuring tool of how well we love God, because one of the ways we show our love to God is by loving and serving his children. King Benjamin taught that "when ye are in the service of your fellow beings ye are only in the service of your God." (Mosiah 2:17.)

We are told that when Christ comes in glory with all of the holy angels, he will sit upon a throne and everyone who ever lived on earth will be gathered before him. Then the Lord will separate the people into two groups: the righteous will be called to stand at his right hand and the others at his left hand. Then Christ, the King, will "say unto them on his right hand, Come, ye blessed of my Father, inherit the kingdom prepared for you from the foundation of the world."

And what is the basis of this glorious ruling? Christlike love expressed through Christian service. "For I was an hungred, and ye gave me meat: I was thirsty, and ye gave me drink: I was a stranger, and ye took me in: Naked, and ye clothed me: I was sick, and ye visited me: I was in prison, and ye came unto me.

"Then shall the righteous answer him, saying, Lord, when

saw we thee an hungred, and fed thee? or thirsty, and gave thee drink? When saw we thee a stranger, and took thee in? or naked, and clothed thee? Or when saw we thee sick, or in prison, and came unto thee?

"And the King shall answer and say unto them, Verily I say unto you, Inasmuch as ye have done it unto one of the least of these my brethren, ye have done it unto me." (Matthew 25:31-40.)

This is a scripture each of us should study carefully. The Lord is explaining to us just how to show our love, both to him and to our spirit brothers and sisters.

We find from other scriptural sources that the Lord meant more than just providing for the temporal means of our brothers and sisters. King Benjamin pleaded with his people,

"Impart of your substance to the poor, every man according to that which he hath, such as feeding the hungry, clothing the naked, visiting the sick and administering to their relief, both *spiritually* and *temporally*, according to their wants." (Mosiah 4:26; italics added.)

Let's take a closer look at how these scriptures can be applied in each of our lives.

I was an hungred, and ye gave me meat

A friend shared how she fed one who was hungry both physically and emotionally:

> The day before Thanksgiving was filled with all of the expected preparations required for a large buffet banquet. At the peak of the day, during the dinner hour, I felt a strong impression to phone a dear friend whose father had passed away just a week ago.
>
> "Are you all right?" I asked with all the sincerity I could express. I really wanted to know and did not want a polite "I'm fine." However, that is exactly what I received from my friend.

"I'm okay," she said distinctly, with hardly any emotion.

"Are you sure you are all right?" I pleaded. "I haven't spoken to you since your father's death last week, and I was worried about you."

"I'm fine!" she retorted with added emphasis.

For some reason, I just wasn't ready to give up. I continued talking as if I hadn't heard her response. I asked her if she'd like to come to my house for Thanksgiving dinner and added a sincere apology for having called her at such short notice with my invitation.

I heard great sighs and then her trembling voice said, "I'd love to come! How can I thank you?" She sobbed and again expressed, *"How* can I ever thank you?" My friend then explained that her son was in another state for the holiday and that she was planning to spend a quiet day resting and catching up on the many items on her "to-do" list, but because of a sudden death of her neighbor down the street, she had felt a strong flood of emotions and confusion. Then she softly added, "Now, because of my own personal battle with health problems, I just don't want to be alone tomorrow."

That was the best "day of thanks and giving" that I think I will ever experience! The food seemed tastier and the cousins seemed to have fewer arguments. The day lasted into the wee hours of the night as my family and friends visited and shared with one another.

In our endeavors to serve God, it is important that we meet the physical needs of others, but hunger and thirst may go even beyond the physical. Philosopher George Jordan suggested that there are "four great hungers of life — body-hunger, mind-hunger, heart-hunger, and soul-hunger. They are all real; all need recognition, all need feeding."

Our friends may hunger and thirst to be given our whole-hearted support, to be listened to, to be understood, to have companionship, to be appreciated, and perhaps most of all to be fed spiritually. When we limit or withhold our acts of love, our friends will feel empty. These feelings may be akin to those described by Isaiah, as quoted by the prophet Nephi in 2 Nephi 27:3: "It shall be unto them, even as unto a hungry man which dreameth, and behold he eateth but he awaketh and his soul is empty; or like unto a thirsty man which dreameth, and behold he drinketh but he awaketh and behold he is faint, and his soul hath appetite." We may feed someone physically, yet leave the person hungry. Truly the acts of feeding physical hunger and quenching physical thirst are necessary. But these experiences in service should prod our understanding to provide more than the physical needs. They can help us learn to fulfill the needs of the inner soul within our friends, to sense the emotional demands, and ultimately to nourish with things of the Spirit. Jesus said, "I am the bread of life: he that cometh to me shall never hunger; and he that believeth on me shall never thirst." (John 6:35.) By sharing the gospel with our friends, we can truly fill their hunger and quench their thirst.

I was a stranger, and ye took me in

There are many different ways in which we can "take in a stranger" and become as a friend. It is important to extend a hand to visitors or new members, active or less active, who enter our ward circle. One Relief Society president told us sadly, "Our ladies are afraid to reach out to people they don't know. There are two inactive sisters who have made a New Year's commitment to start coming to church. They have been coming for three weeks now, and both sit all alone on the back row. No one talks to them and no one sits by them. Last week one of the new sisters stayed out in the hall because she felt so left out."

It takes only a moment to stretch forth a hand to a stranger and make an introduction. That moment of warmth may be an investment in her eternity. Sisters sitting alone in meetings should hear the soothing tones of, "Come and sit by me."

And how blessed is the sister who sees one all alone and leaves her friends to offer companionship to the stranger. Many Latter-day Saints who have a testimony of the gospel of Jesus Christ stay home from church because they do not feel the fellowship of the Saints.

Paul said, "Now therefore ye are no more strangers and foreigners, but fellowcitizens with the saints, and of the household of God." (Ephesians 2:19.) We can accept the challenge to see every person who sets foot in our ward building feels like a friend and not a foreigner. But we can't "take in" a stranger unless we can truly care about her and love that stranger as Heavenly Father loves each of us.

Naked, and ye clothed me

The following story illustrates a unique way that one sister found to "clothe the naked":

A good friend of mine suddenly found herself with the challenge of raising a new family — her two abused grandchildren — after all her children were grown and gone. Her grandchildren were over the age of eight and had never been baptized, so one of the first things my friend did was help them prepare for this sacred event in their lives.

Soon all the arrangements were made and everything seemed well organized. The children were to wear some white baptismal jumpsuits that were stored in the church closet; hence, on Saturday morning, my friend went to the church to get the jumpsuits. To her dismay, the white clothes were not there. No one seemed to know why or how the jumpsuits came up missing, but they couldn't be located anywhere.

Shortly after her distressing discovery I called my friend at home. Sensing the stress and anxiety in her voice, I asked, "Is anything wrong?"

She explained the problem, adding, "I just don't know what I am going to do!"

As I tried to calm her down, I remembered that I had several yards of white material (I keep a ten years' supply of material along with my food storage, much to the dismay of my clutter-conscious husband!) and had recently purchased a basic children's jumpsuit pattern (I don't know why; it just seemed like the thing to do at the time).

"It will only take me a few hours to sew the two outfits," I told my friend. "I will deliver the jumpsuits to the church in time for the baptismal service." Then I added, "Don't worry. I won't let you down."

I sewed the jumpsuits, delivered them on time, and completely forgot about the entire experience until recently when my parents handed me a letter that had been written to them years ago by this same grandmother-friend shortly after her grandchildren's baptism. In the letter, my friend told my parents about the incident and what I had done for her when she felt so desperate and alone, and how I had given her an assurance by my actions of the "great love our Heavenly Father has for each of us by sending friends to help when we seemingly need it the most."

I was overwhelmed by my friend's gratitude over something that had been just ordinary and seemingly inconsequential to me at the time, but now I realize that it was a growing experience in learning to clothe with love.

How often do we feel "naked" and bare when we are without love? In a revelation given to the Prophet Joseph Smith, the Lord commanded, "And above all things, clothe yourselves with the bond of charity, as with a mantle, which is the bond of perfectness and peace." (D&C 88:125.) If we clothe ourselves with charity we will freely clothe others with the "pure love of Christ," for that is what charity is. (Moroni 7:47.)

I was sick, and ye visited me

Not only can we visit the sick, but we can go the extra mile in bringing them comfort, as this experience shows:

> Shortly before our last stake conference, the bishop announced that we would be blessed with a visit from an apostle and two other General Authorities at our stake conference. I asked the bishop if he was planning to ask the brethren to visit a sweet sister and friend who had been almost totally confined to her bed for the past nine years; if he hadn't considered it, would he please try to arrange the visit? He responded, "I will do what I can," and I assumed that was the end of my hopes. I didn't dare say a word to my friend about the possibility of the Brethren visiting her; I didn't want to get her excited about something that probably wouldn't happen.
>
> Sunday, after conference, I timidly entered her bedroom. My friend was lying down, but instead of hearing her usual happy greeting, I found her wiping tears from her eyes. Wondering if something awful had happened, I asked anxiously, "What's wrong?"
>
> She clasped her hands together and sighed, "You'll never guess what has happened!"
>
> Worried, I quickly responded, "Oh, no! What?"
>
> With more tears flowing freely down her cheeks she said, with much difficulty, "This afternoon, Elder _____ and two other General Authorities, along with the stake president and our bishop, came to my bedroom. They visited with me and put their hands on my head and gave me the most wonderful

15

blessing! This has been the most special day of my entire life!"

Quickly, I sat at my friend's side and hugged her and we both continued to shed many tears of joy over the gospel that we shared and loved. What a difference the blessings of the gospel experienced and shared with a friend can make in our sojourn on earth!

It is important to visit those who are physically sick, but we need also to remember those who are spiritually sick. The scriptures tell us, "But their scribes and Pharisees murmured against his disciples, saying, Why do ye eat and drink with publicans and sinners? And Jesus answering said unto them, They that are whole need not a physician; but they that are sick. I came not to call the righteous, but sinners to repentance." (Luke 5:30-32.) Many times a Relief Society president will hear the plea, "Please don't send me to any inactive sisters." But part of our calling as visiting teachers is to visit and comfort those who are spiritually ailing.

I was in prison, and ye came unto me

Hollie Bevan had an unusual experience uplifting a soul in prison:

A few years ago my neighbor called to ask if my husband and I would serve as witnesses at her wedding. In addition, she asked if I would be the pianist and also provide a special musical selection during the ceremony. "I know I am asking a lot, but there are rules limiting the number of people that I can invite to the wedding. The marriage," she continued to explain, "will take place in the prison chapel."

My friend's fiancé had been in prison for a number of months, and because there were children involved, they had finally decided to make their union legal in the eyes of the law, for fear that if they continued as they were, the courts might step in and remove their children from the home.

Their lifestyle was definitely foreign to my own, and I had to struggle with my emotions and attitudes to rid myself of any horrid judgments. After much prayer for strength to keep my attitude as one in which I felt the Lord would share, I was able to happily offer my help. I thanked my Heavenly Father that she had trusted me enough to come to me, opening a door for friendship and the gospel. I deeply sensed the great responsibility of being an instrument in the hands of God.

The Lord will use us to assist in reaching out to his children if we are willing to respond, even if that response takes us to a prison. But in reality "prison" is more than a physical place; it's also a state without the gospel and without charity. Prison can be the bars of negative feelings and thoughts. Some are imprisoned by drugs, alcohol, and sins. Others have spirits that are imprisoned in unhealthy bodies.

As always, Christ showed us the way through his example. When Paul was in prison, "the Lord stood by him, and said, Be of good cheer, Paul." (Acts 23:11.) Many are imprisoned by their fears or by depression; We too can stand by them and help them to "be of good cheer."

The Lord also "visited, and preached the gospel" unto "spirits of men kept in prison." (D&C 76:73.) When we perform sacred ordinances in the temple we are being friends to our sisters and brothers on the other side of the veil, who are literally in prison and cannot progress until their temple work is done. Joseph Fielding Smith taught, "We have the privilege of acting vicariously for the dead, in performing the ordinances which pertain to this life. They who go into the spirit world, who hold the priesthood of God, teach the dead the everlasting gospel in the spirit world; and when the dead are willing to repent and receive those teachings, and the work is done for them here vicariously, they shall have the privilege of coming out of the prison house to find their place in the kingdom of God."

Paul instructed church members of his time and ours, "By love serve one another. For all the law is fulfilled in one word, even in this; Thou shalt love thy neighbour as thyself." (Galatians 5:13-14.) James, the half-brother of the Lord, calls the second commandment the "royal law." (See James 2:8.) The Lord promises the greatest of all gifts to those who learn to live the second commandment and thereby also live the first and great commandment: he promises us *eternal life.*

CHAPTER 3

Love Encircles Through Support

To give someone support means to help lift heavy burdens, to encourage, to uphold when others may tear down, to bear with and endure all phases of life, and, on stage and many times in real life, to have a role subordinate to the "star." Add to that "wholehearted," which means with all one's energy and enthusiasm. Our Heavenly Father gives wholehearted support to his children. King Benjamin taught that God is "preserving you from day to day, by lending you breath, that ye may live and move and do according to your own will, and even supporting you from one moment to another." (Mosiah 2:21.) Satan, the great enemy of love, leads people in his dark paths, but in the end, Alma cautioned us to see clearly that "the devil will not support his children at the last day, but doth speedily drag them down to hell." (Alma 30:60.) Those who wish to encircle others with love must be willing to follow God's example of wholehearted support.

Hollie received this kind of support from two wonderful friends, Dean and Zella. They called and invited her over for dinner, refusing her offers to contribute to the meal. They even provided a baby-sitter for her children. When she arrived at their house, their bubbly attitude was a little puzzling to her. She explains:

My friends greeted me at their front door with
an enthusiasm and excitement that was almost con-
tagious. Then I saw the reason for this specific
treatment. There, seated at the dining room table,
was a *male!* They had set me up on a blind dinner
date without even telling me about their plans be-
forehand! I wanted to feel embarrassed, but I
couldn't because my friends were so proud of me
and so busy expounding my good qualities to the
young man, that I didn't have time to squeeze any
disgruntled emotions from my heart.

Dean and Zella also didn't seem to be the least
bit concerned about my physical state: I was eight
months pregnant and also just recently divorced.
Instead they expressed their love and admiration for
me to the mystery man as if I was someone really
special.

I was amazed at how successfully my friends had
pulled off this caper. And what's even more important, it proved to be a wonderful boost for my poor
self-image. I didn't feel fat and dumpy anymore, but
instead I felt like an attractive young woman with
much to offer.

Dean and Zella had the talent of giving wholehearted support.
Because of this, they were able to lift Hollie in a way that most
of us wouldn't even dare to approach. The rest of us, who are
learning this skill "line upon line, precept upon precept, here a
little and there a little" (2 Nephi 28:30), can learn a lot by
studying their example. Dean and Zella's wholehearted support
reached into three critical areas of need: physical, emotional,
and spiritual. They had not only treated Hollie to a meal that
was beyond her meager means and supplied her with a baby-sitter
for a special night away from her feelings of loneliness, but they
had included in their actions and words a love toward her that
caused her to feel, nothing doubting, that she is a beloved daugh-
ter of God.

Following Dean and Zella's example, we'll further illustrate how each of us can give wholehearted support in our own efforts to love others.

Physical support

Hollie loves to tell this story of a time when Zella offered her physical support:

> My friend Zella and I were taking some classes together at the local university. On one particularly bad winter morning, with snow and ice everywhere, Zella picked me up in her car and courageously drove up the hill to the Utah State University, parking her car in the first available lot. Looking around, we realized that the entire perimeter of the parking lot was covered with a huge wall of ice and snow — the work of the university snow removal team the night before. Zella surveyed the situation and found a place that had melted down to about three feet high. She hopped up and over the ice because, as usual, she was appropriately dressed in pants and snow boots. I, in my dress and spike-heeled boots, was not faring so well. I cautiously began with only two steps up the ice, but instead of going forward, I slid back down.
>
> "Hollie, hurry up! We're going to be late for class."
>
> I heard a note of impatience in Zella's voice and forced myself to take three steps, but to no avail; I slid backwards to the bottom of the ice again. It was obvious that I needed some help.
>
> Zella hopped to the top of that ice "Matter-horn," grabbed my hands, and began skiing me up the slope. This worked fantastically until I neared the top. My knees suddenly buckled and my feet started to slide in opposite directions.
>
> "Don't move!" Zella yelled.

Actually, I wasn't about to go anywhere. My future plans didn't include falling on my bottom and wearing a wet skirt to class! Luckily for me Zella didn't leave me stranded, as the next moment I discovered that she had maneuvered herself behind me and somehow had begun bulldozing my broadside up the peak with the back of her shoulders. It must have looked as though I was sitting on top of her head! Zella continued to push me to the top of the ice, which made me feel very confident and much relieved until I realized that I wasn't stopping at the top, but instead was losing my balance and beginning to nose dive toward the other side.

In the very nick of time, Zella grabbed the hem of my dress and with all of her one-hundred-and-five-pound might she pulled my body back into an upright position. Then she hopped, skipped, and jumped back over the ice to position herself in front of me. Walking in front of me like my guardian angel, she assisted me with my slippery-soled boots down that other side until I was safely at the bottom and could balance myself with confidence. As we proudly turned to continue on our way, we discovered students encircling us who had stopped to watch the entire show.

To this very day, I can't recall whether or not Zella and I even made it to class, but I will never forget that great example she instilled in me as to the lengths she was willing to go to in order to help me physically over an icy barrier.

Most of us will never have the opportunity to pull someone over an ice mountain, but we will have other chances to show concern and care in physical matters. Traditionally, as Relief Society sisters, our main focus has been on meal preparations, housecleaning, and laundry, but there are many other ways to help those in need. You can be creative in your gifts of love to the bedridden. For instance, you could supply them with favorite books and tapes filled with light, humorous anecdotes to help make the days brighter. If you are talented in crafts you could share your skills with someone who is confined. Counted cross-stitch, ceramics, knitting, needlepoint, quilting, and other skills can make the time pass more quickly and give the homebound person a feeling of accomplishment.

When people are confined to their houses or beds for long periods of time there are problems of "missing." They miss their children's ward and school activities, concerts, games, and plays. If you have a video camera or cassette tape recorder you could tape some of these special events. You might also volunteer to act as a shuttle service or to be a surrogate mother at children's functions.

Flowers help cheer up the sick. You can share a variety from your own garden. It is always a good idea to use a container that doesn't have to be returned, such as a plastic ice cream bucket. Lauren shared a single iris with five buds on it with her bedridden friend. The friend watched each purple flower slowly curl back and then burst open. "What a miracle!" the friend exclaimed. "Never in all my life have I had time to watch a flower bloom." Then the friend chuckled, "And I hope that never in all my life will I have the time again!"

The homebound person also misses out on church meetings. Again, you could offer to tape record these events. Hearing the prayers, songs, announcements, lessons, and comments can help a person who cannot attend feel closer and more a part of things.

These are only a few ways in which you can show physical support. The most important point to understand is that good intentions must be spurred on to positive action. You must physically be there to meet physical needs. Your willingness to sacrifice and serve translates into great expressions of love to the recipient.

Emotional support

Emotional support differs from physical support. This type of support happens when we listen without making judgments and when we love without imposing any conditions. When we do this, we "lift up the hands which hang down, and strengthen the feeble knees." (D&C 81:5.)

Hollie had a precious opportunity to provide emotional support to one in need:

> One night I received a phone call from the bishop. "I need you to come over to my office immediately." He didn't explain or offer any reasons, but I knew by the tone of his voice that it was urgent. Since I lived just across the street from the church, I found myself knocking on his office door within minutes of his call.
>
> The bishop came out to greet me, quietly closing the office door behind him. "Hollie," he said softly, "I have a young teenage girl in my office whom I have just stopped from completing a suicide attempt. Her parents are on their way, but it will be nearly four hours before they arrive. Could you please take her home and love her?"
>
> I felt my throat swell into a knot, and my heart started thumping through my blouse. The only way I could answer him was to nod yes.
>
> When he opened his office door, I saw a young girl whose eyes were swollen and beet-red. Her facial muscles were drawn and molded into a mask that kept her from having direct eye contact with anyone. She looked so forlorn and dismal, so broken down, that in the first instant when she walked through the doorway I found myself immediately feeling great compassion and love toward her.
>
> "Hollie, this is . . . well, we'll just call her Jane," whispered the bishop. "She's prepared to go with you now."
>
> I reached out and lightly patted her shoulder and my touch seemed to push a button in her soul. She responded by looking up at me with an expression in her eyes that pleaded, "Please help me!"

Pointing the direction to proceed, I nudged her elbow and we walked in silence back to my house. As we entered, my children rushed out of bed, excited about having a visitor in the house. "Would you like to help me get them back into bed?" I asked Jane with apprehension, and she instantly nodded yes, without uttering a word. As we were tucking them into bed, my little ones reached up and hugged Jane, each in turn expressing their good nights with, "Sweet dreams, Jane, I love you."

Jane didn't say a word but lovingly gave each child a bear-type hug. In fact, she clung to each one as if she were afraid to let go. Then, with tears in her eyes, she turned to look at me, searching my face for needed approval. I winked and smiled, and Jane smiled back at me. I suggested that we go to the kitchen and just talk.

"Oh, I forgot that I'm supposed to bake cookies for tomorrow," I mentioned, breaking the silence. "Jane, would you like to help me bake chocolate chip cookies?"

"Can we eat some, too?" she responded with a sudden excitement in her expression.

We spent the next four hours talking, baking, crying, eating, and laughing, until at 11 P.M., the phone rang and ended our giggly cookie party. It was the bishop. Jane's parents had arrived.

Jane and I walked quickly across the street to the church. There was a definite bounce in her stride now, not like the slow, heavy steps she had taken on her way to my house earlier in the evening. We found the bishop waiting outside his office door for us, his face glowing as he watched us coming down the long hall toward him. As we came within speaking distance, he greeted us with, "Hello, hello!" and then cautiously added, "Well, Jane, how do you feel?"

"I'm okay," she responded with a note of confidence.

The bishop then quickly escorted her into his office, where her parents waited nervously for her appearance. Standing all alone outside in the hall, I felt quite lost for a moment, not knowing what I should do, but soon the bishop reappeared. He patted my shoulder, and with a wink in his watery eyes, he softly reassured me. "She's going to be all right. She has a *friend.*"

With sudden realization, I truly understood the message in his simple response. He was referring to me — I was Jane's friend. Not because of common interests, but because I cared. And in my caring, I also helped Jane to realize how much the Savior cared and that he is her friend.

When someone needs emotional support, we must keep the door of communication wide open. If Hollie had lectured Jane, splashing her with moral judgments and verbal platitudes, she would not have been able to have built a friendship with her. As depressed and lonely as Jane felt within herself, she needed most of all to know that someone cared and understood her feelings. Hollie's role at that time was to reassure Jane and demonstrate her friendship by sincerely listening with heartfelt empathy, to help her bear her "infirmities." (See Romans 15:1-2, 5.) With this approach, it didn't take long for an emotional bond of trust to develop between them, which then allowed Hollie to help Jane climb out of her pit of despair and loneliness.

Elder Robert L. Simpson related the following:

"During the past twelve months it has been my privilege to work closely with many emotionally disturbed people; others who have transgressed; some who have found themselves out of harmony with society; still others who were lonely and afraid. It has not been a year of discouragement and despair, however, because the vast majority of these people have made an important decision, and they have said, 'I want to change my life. I am ready to take direction from someone who really cares. . . . '

"Every success story of the past year has been the result of special effort on the part of the people who cared. They cared enough . . . to follow the great example set by the Savior." (Taken from the *Ensign*, July 1973, pp. 22-23.)

Spiritual support

The greatest teacher who ever lived, our Savior, said, "Love one another, as I have loved you." (John 15:12.) The Apostle Peter was taught the importance of spiritual support when Jesus asked him not once, but three times, "Simon, son of Jonas, lovest thou me?" Peter answered with wholehearted sincerity "Lord, thou knowest all things; thou knowest that I love thee." And Jesus answered him, "Feed my sheep." (John 21:15-17.) Christ was not telling Peter to provide His flock with physical food. His message had reference to Peter's commission and responsibility to give spiritual nourishment. The prophet Alma explained this responsibility to his son Helaman: "I have labored without ceasing, . . . that I might bring them to taste of the exceeding joy of which I did taste; that they might also be born of God, and be filled with the Holy Ghost." (Alma 36:24.)

We spiritually nourish others when we learn to value them for who they really are. We must look beyond outward appearances (wealth, position, beauty, talents, and so on) or considerations of what they can do for us, and recognize their inherent worth as sons and daughters of God. With this knowledge we are in a position to lift and support others spiritually. Elder Robert L. Simpson has reminded us that "the Savior did not seem to be so much involved in giving money. You will remember that his gifts were in the form of personal attention, in performing an administration, and in sharing the gifts of the Spirit."

As we follow the example of our greatest friend, our Savior, we should watch for moments where we can be instruments in inspiring others spiritually. One of the best tools we have for this task is prayer, as illustrated in the following story:

I have a friend who, through a very serious illness, seemed to be losing control of her emotions

27

and even her sane judgment. It was during this very painful and trying time as I sat by her bed just holding her hand and watching her drift away that she looked up and asked, "Will you pray for me?"

I responded emphatically, "I have been praying both morning and night for you."

"No, I mean will you pray with me, now?" she pleaded, and added with fervor, "Please help me!"

I knelt down at her side and together we prayed to our Heavenly Father. A sweetness came over her and as we wept together, I watched her countenance change before my eyes as she gained hope. She became passive and calm and a peace bore her up as she endured the suffering encountered on her road to recovery.

Just as our Savior prayed for his disciples while he was here on earth, we too should pray for each other; as he loves us with an unconditional love, we too can respond unconditionally; and as he is true, loyal, and faithful, we too can learn to show these attributes.

One of the exciting things about encircling others with love is that you don't have to wait to be asked to help. It doesn't matter whether a person needs physical help, emotional support, or spiritual uplifting, as long as *you* respond to the signals, often silent pleas for help, with comfort and edification. (See 1 Thessalonians 5:11.)

We are often prompted with small feelings and ideas that would benefit a sister or brother in need of support. In fact, President Harold B. Lee said, "Every soul [in the Church] who has been blessed to receive the Holy Ghost has the power to receive revelation. God help you and me that we will always so live that the Lord can answer the prayers of the faithful through us in our good deeds." By listening to the Spirit, we can be instruments in encircling others in the arms of the Lord's love.

Our friend Paula Smith tells how she received spiritual support from caring neighbors:

I was really active when I was growing up. After I was married, we moved around a lot. At first, I tried to attend my church meetings, but no one reached out to me. I didn't feel really welcome; in fact, I felt out of place. Then we moved again. The people in my new neighborhood were very warm and friendly. Almost immediately, my husband and I had all kinds of friends. One woman visited with me several times. We would just sit in my living room and chat. One afternoon she announced, "Oh, by the way, I'm your visiting teacher." After several more visits she decided to give me the visiting teaching message. Later she invited me to attend Relief Society and gave me the meeting schedule. I decided to attend. Many of my neighbors were there and I felt loved and accepted at once. It wasn't long after I started going to church again that I was called to be a visiting teacher, then the sewing specialist. We lived in that ward for four and a half years, and as my testimony grew I received other callings: visiting teacher coordinator, second counselor in the Primary, and Primary president.

Then came the opportunity to buy our first home. I was excited, yet sad and a little frightened. I was sure that it would never be the same and that I would never find friends as wonderful as the ones I was leaving. When I expressed these feelings to my friends they said, "Heavenly Father knows your needs and everything is going to be all right." So I spent a lot of time on my knees praying, "Heavenly Father, please help me to find somebody who will understand my needs and who I can be close to."

We moved in on a Saturday and on the following Monday Bret and Lauren Leifson came over and brought us a loaf of banana bread. As they sat and visited with us I told Lauren that a lot of our things

were still in boxes in the garage. The conversation
continued on and I didn't think anything else about
it. When Bret and Lauren got ready to leave she
said, "I will be over tomorrow at 10:00."

That will be great, I thought, *but why?*

Lauren must have seen that I was puzzled so she
added quickly, "To help you unpack."

When Lauren and Bret left I started to cry. I
knew that Heavenly Father had answered my prayers.

In this example Lauren was able to meet Paula's physical
needs by offering to help her unpack, her emotional needs by
giving comfort in a time of stressful upheaval, and her spiritual
needs by being the answer to Paula's prayer and thus strengthening
Paula's testimony. When we are directed by the Holy Ghost
we will always be able to accomplish more than we can on our
own.

It is important always to act upon those little promptings
and impressions that you receive. Whether you feel an impression
to send a short note to a friend, or the sudden urge to stop at a
friend's home or office unannounced, decide now not to miss
any opportunities to show love. Don't dismiss that feeling—act
on it!

When we choose to give our wholehearted support to others
we will be aware of their temporal needs, take their hands and
walk a few steps with them when they are emotionally down-
trodden, and offer spiritual support through prayers and sharing
the gospel, reminding them that, above all, they are children of
God.

CHAPTER 4

The Gift of Time

You may agree with the concepts we've discussed so far, but wonder despairingly, "Where do you find the time?" If so, you are not alone. Our Church leaders frequently remind us that we should read our scriptures, keep a journal, pray morning and night, attend meetings (we could spend an entire paragraph listing all the different types of meetings), do temple work, sing in the ward choir, prepare family home evenings, participate in weekly activity nights, lengthen our stride in performing our church callings, do genealogy . . . the responsibilities go on and on, and we have included only the demands of being a member of the Church. We are not even going to try to list work and home responsibilities. When the Lord said, "Thou shalt not idle away thy time" (D&C 60:13), he meant it!

Time is precious. No matter what your time constraints are, you must understand this: time is essential to forming loving relationships. A gift of time says, "You are important to me." People learn that they are valuable when others take time to listen to them, talk to them, and be with them.

Following are some suggestions on how to use effectively the little time you have in reaching out to other people.

1. Change your "I'm too busy" attitude. Without realizing it you may be silently broadcasting a "busy signal" to everyone around you. If you want people to know they are an important part of your life, you can't keep putting them on hold until you have time.

One sister suggested a possible plan:

> I noticed that when friends and family called
> me they would preface their conversation with, "I
> know you're really busy, but . . . " or "I know you
> don't have time to talk but this will only take a sec-
> ond." This bothered me. After a lot of thought, I
> decided that I didn't want people to feel like they
> were being squeezed into a tight, inflexible schedule.
> But how could I convey this, when my time was
> very limited? Finally I decided on a simple plan. In
> the future when I received the usual "I know you're
> busy" preface, I would answer cheerfully, "Not at
> all! I would love to talk!" People immediately be-
> came more relaxed and responded with great
> warmth, and most often, the conversation was only
> a few moments longer than it would have been
> when I was letting everyone know what a hyper-
> pace I traveled. It was a small gesture on my part,
> but it made a difference to those around me.

When people ask you to do them a favor, try saying, "I would
be happy to," or "I would love to do that for you." If you are
willing to do the job, it requires no more effort to be enthusiastic
than it does to mumble, "I guess so." This small change of attitude
will create warm feelings of love and friendship.

One sister makes it a point to ask, "What can I do for you?"
when someone calls her on the phone, thus offering help before
she has to be asked. When this woman offers her assistance, she
plans to serve. If she is turned down she says, "How do you
expect me to get any blessings in the kingdom if you don't let
me help you?" Her generous attitude makes the receiver feel
comfortable.

Christ said, "And whosoever shall compel thee to go a mile,
go with him twain." (Matthew 5:41.) Surely the Lord does not
want us to grumble and complain about how busy we are and
how much time the detour is taking, as we walk that extra mile!

2. Remember the importance of little things. Small acts of kindness, which require only brief amounts of time, can help make people feel important in your life and may even spark great new friendships. Lord Chesterfield stated, "Trifles, little attentions, mere nothings, either done or neglected, will make you either liked or disliked in the general run of the world." Alma, said, "By small and simple things are great things brought to pass." (Alma 37:6.)

It takes very little effort to raise your hand and wave to a passing acquaintance when you are driving down the road. Add a broad smile and that person will know you are genuinely glad to see him or her. Perhaps this will begin a friendship. At the very least it will brighten someone's day.

Taking the time to give a compliment is a little kindness with lasting effects. Lauren remembers a great lesson taught her by a friend:

> A friend once gave me some advice: If there is ever anything, no matter how insignificant, that impresses you about another person, tell them, *and tell them immediately!* I didn't understand just how good this counsel was until it had a personal effect on my life. During one Christmas season, my husband and I attended a party where I had been asked to lead the caroling. Knowing I would be in front of a large group, I wanted to look my best that evening. An hour before the party started, I was home frantically pulling clothes out of my closet.
>
> "I don't have anything to wear!" I cried. I guess I was hoping that right at that moment my mate would pull out a beautifully wrapped package containing a new dress, complete with matching jewelry, shoes, and purse. Why not? It happened to Cinderella.
>
> Coming back down to reality, I quickly pulled on a blue skirt and pink blouse and we drove to the party. I felt extremely uncomfortable and unhappy

as we approached the door. Over and over again a
little voice in my mind said, "You look terrible."

As we entered the room, Glenna, the hostess,
greeted us. "You look really nice, Lauren," she
commented.

Immediately my spirits lifted and the little voice
went silent.

"Do you really think so?" I asked hopefully.

"Yes, I do. I think you look wonderful."

I gave her a quick squeeze and thanked her. It
was such a simple act, to give a compliment, but
my outlook for the evening brightened and I thor-
oughly enjoyed the Christmas party. Her small act
of kindness elevated my self-esteem at a time when
I needed it.

By now you have probably realized that we are talking about
the everyday, humdrum circumstances that we face over and over
again. Waving, talking on the phone, and offering compliments
are not occasions that make sparks fly. But keep in mind that
relationships usually begin slowly and blossom at ordinary moments while people are doing ordinary things. Friendships may
start over such seemingly insignificant things as stopping to talk
across the fence, chatting for a minute in the grocery store, taking
cookies to a new neighbor, offering to baby-sit a friend's children,
giving someone a hug, taking a break at work with a co-worker,
or making a newcomer feel welcome at a meeting.

A thank-you note is another small gesture that makes a big
difference. Just because most friendships blossom in everyday
circumstances, that doesn't mean that we can't put a little of the
unusual and unexpected in a relationship. Square, printed cards
are nice and formal, but a thank-you note could also be an
opportunity to use a little imagination. Wouldn't it be fun to
receive a thank-you card in secret code? (Of course, the decoding
solution would have to be attached to it or the thank you could
turn out to be a real frustration.) Send a note inside a balloon
or attached to a flower. Saying thank you can be just as much fun
as receiving the kindness or gift.

Small gestures can become opportunities to make friends and strengthen relationships.

3. Learn to do two things at a time. What do you usually do with your friends—go to lunch, right? That's great, but there are so many other things you can do that would give you a chance to spend time with someone and accomplish a personal goal too. Be creative! Invite a friend to do a service project with you, such as visiting a shut-in person or fellowshipping a neighbor. One of our friends organized a flower-planting party for a neighbor who had been confined to bed. She gathered together several people in the neighborhood. They brought their weed-eaters and work gloves and pooled their money to purchase two flats of petunias. In two hours the yard was weeded, trimmed, and planted with gorgeous flowers that the sick friend could enjoy all summer long, and the experience gave those neighbors who participated a chance to get to know each other better.

Exercise is one of those things we all need to do, but for many of us, the only thing that gets a workout is our guilty conscience. Ask a neighbor to walk, jog, or do aerobics with you.

Offer rides to firesides, ward temple nights, PTA meetings, and so on. Doubling up not only saves gas money, but it gives people time to socialize. Study your scriptures with a friend. Invite another family over for family home evening or activity night; ask them to furnish the dessert or the lesson, and then trade on another night. Ask a friend to help you with genealogy or, if you have this skill, offer your help. Hollie invited friends and family over for a Thanksgiving feast and then added, "Bring your box of genealogy. We are going to work on it after dinner."

Home chores can be performed faster when the burden is shared by two. Ask a neighbor to come over for a canning session. Divide the cost and split the fruit of your labors. Organize an old-fashioned quilting bee. Think how much fun it would be to gather together friends and make a quilt for each one in turn.

Lauren grew up in a family of ten brothers and sisters. One of the family responsibilities in her home was for each child to wash dishes on an assigned night of the week. You can imagine how long it took with thirteen plates, thirteen sets of silverware, pots, pans, serving dishes, and so on. Lauren's grandmother was living with them at the time, and after each meal she would get up and begin clearing the table. It created a great feeling of guilt to have an eighty-nine-year-old woman help with the dishes, so Lauren would say, "Grandma, you really don't need to help. Why don't you sit down and rest?" Her grandmother would smile and sing, "Many hands make light work." She was right, and not only did the dishes get done more quickly, but Lauren and her grandmother had time to chat for a while.

4. Take time to listen to the Spirit. The Holy Ghost will guide and direct you in filling the urgent and necessary needs of people.

When Jill discovered on April Fool's Day 1987 that she was going to have twins, the doctor put her to bed for the remaining two months of her pregnancy. Jill remembers:

> One very long and lonely day, I lay in bed with the blinds closed. The room was dark and so were my thoughts. I constantly worried about the babies. "What if they come early? What if they are too small and have to stay in the hospital? What if they have birth defects? What if they die . . . " I knew where these fears were coming from, yet they would not leave.
>
> Suddenly, the door burst open and there was my friend Diane. "I don't have very much time," she said, almost breathlessly. "I was just driving down the street and had the feeling that you needed a hug." She reached down and grabbed my shoulders and gave me the warmest, most wonderful hug. I melted in her arms and started to cry. In a few minutes I had poured out all of my fears and my friend took them in and promised to store them for me. "Don't worry. Everything will be all right," she promised.
>
> Diane was there for only five minutes, yet I felt comforted.

Elder Boyd K. Packer said, "I have come to know that inspiration comes more as a feeling than a sound." Diane did not hear a voice, yet she had a feeling that Jill needed a hug. Many people dismiss this kind of feeling, saying, "I don't know if it is coming from me or the Holy Ghost." It is easy to tell. Mormon gave us the key. "Wherefore, all things which are good cometh of God; and that which is evil cometh of the devil . . . that which is of God inviteth and enticeth to do good continually; wherefore, every thing which inviteth and enticeth to do good, and to love God, and to serve him, is inspired of God." (Moroni 7:12-13.)

So if you have a feeling you need to call someone, or write, or visit, no matter how busy you are, no matter what you are doing, act on those feelings; they come from the Spirit and will always be the right thing to do.

Investing our time in people will always bring great returns. Acts of kindness are generally accepted gratefully and usually returned tenfold. Lauren talks about an investment of time she made that really paid off:

> Several months ago we invited a friend over for dinner. She called me a few hours before she was to come and asked if she could bring some Icelandic halibut. My husband and I love fish, so I quickly assured her it would be great. That was my first reward: she was bringing the main course. The second reward came when my friend arrived: she even cooked the fish for us. We had a very enjoyable evening together and she insisted that we keep the leftover fish to enjoy for dinner the next day. The third reward: no cooking tomorrow.
>
> The next afternoon my sister stopped by to visit. I told her about the fabulous fish we had enjoyed the night before and offered her some to take home for dinner. When I pulled the plate out of the refrigerator and lifted up the foil covering, there were only two small pieces left.

"Whoops, I thought there was more left over than this," I apologized. "Since I've bragged about how good it is, why don't you take what's left. We had plenty of it last night and I want you to taste it." My sister thanked me and left.

"Boy, that was dumb," I said to myself. "Now what are you going to have for dinner?" I looked in the freezer. "I guess the menu for tonight is frozen burritos," I said out loud.

Two hours later the phone rang. It was my neighbor. I was surprised to hear from her since I knew she was in the middle of packing to move to another city.

"I was wondering if you wanted to have our old dining room set. We just bought a new one and we don't have room in our new house for this one. Would you be interested?"

I glanced over at our sixty-year-old, bright yellow and silver chromed dining room table, which we had purchased used just before we were married five years ago.

"Yes," I exclaimed. "You have no idea how much we need it." (Afterwards I thought that she certainly did have an idea how much we needed it. She had been in my kitchen many times.)

The fourth reward: a new dining room set! Now, you may tell me long and loud that inviting a friend over to dinner had no direct cause-and-effect relation on the fact that we ended up with a new dining room set, but you would never convince me. As someone once said (slightly paraphrasing the Bible), "Cast your bread upon the waters and it will come back to you toasted and buttered."

Time is our most precious commodity. It is an asset, just like money. When you give someone your time, it is the highest compliment you can pay them. In effect you are saying, "I think you are worthwhile." So give the gift of time to people. You never know what rewards will come your way or whose day you might brighten. You might even find that the sunshine you bring will brighten your own day.

CHAPTER 5

Foes to Love

Women should be allies: showing love, building up, and lifting each other. Unfortunately sometimes just the opposite is true: we pick at, gossip, pull down, and judge. We need to recognize what a great force our nurturing nature can be in helping build the self-worth of those around us. Often, women see themselves through the eyes of other women. If they feel that they are loved and respected, then they are more able to love and respect themselves. It takes a strong foundation of confidence and self-esteem for all women to go forward and accomplish their missions here on earth. You can help strengthen those foundations or help to destroy them.

First let's look at some common problems that are damaging to loving relationships.

Cicero cautioned, "Never injure a friend, even in jest." Sarcasm and "put-downs" are sometimes deadly. Week after week we watch this carefully cultivated type of humor on TV sit-coms, which joke about fat people, dumb people, ugly people, clumsy people, aging people, and so on. The canned audience laughs and we are programmed to think that these jokes are funny. But in the real world, sometimes they are not funny. Often they hurt!

Jokes about ethnic groups, such as the once-popular and frequently resurrected "Polack" jokes, sometimes offend people. One of our friends is a generation removed from her Polish heritage. She literally wilts during the telling of one of these types of jokes. As the room erupts in laughter she ducks her head and stares down at her feet to hide her embarrassment and anger. After following the struggles of the courageous Polish people to remain free even though oppressed by their communist neighbors, we too feel great indignation when this type of joke is told.

Jokes that make fun of physical problems and handicaps are also offensive, as one friend's experience shows:

> One evening I listened to the telling of a joke that involved a person with a "harelip." We all snickered as the joke master spoke in a nasal-toned twang—well, almost all of us. There was one young lady who was edging her way to the outside of the group. When our eyes met I saw great sadness and then I remembered that she has a brother that was born with a cleft palate and a harelip. To her, the joke was cruel.

Jokes about tragedies such as death, disease, divorce, and disasters are also bound to hurt someone. As Shakespeare so aptly put it, "He jests at scars that never felt a wound."

Are there any funny jokes that don't hurt people? Yes! Erma Bombeck takes everyday irritations and situations and finds the humor in them. Instead of putting down other people, she laughs at herself. She becomes a mirror to our personalities and we, in turn, laugh out loud when we see our own reflections through her humor. In other words, if you want to share with the world your most embarrassing moment, or highlight your own bulging waistline, or make jokes about your midlife crisis, or tell a story about your foibles, go right ahead. Hollie once told a friend, "I got up at 5:30 A.M. to do my gardening, but my allergies became so bad I just had to go right in the house and remove my false eyelashes."

Her friend laughed for months thinking about Hollie out gardening in full dress makeup. "If I can't joke about my vanity, I might really start taking it seriously," Hollie often quips.

There is nothing wrong with putting yourself in the spotlight of humor, but be aware that there are some very sensitive people (and sometimes people who are not so sensitive, but have very tender spots in their human makeup) who don't appreciate it if you shed any rays in their direction.

Solomon Freehof once said, "Years ago I preferred clever people. There was joy in beholding . . . a mind . . . bearing thought quickly translated into words, or ideas expressed in a new way. I find now that my taste has changed. Verbal fireworks often bore me. They seem motivated by self-assertion and self-display. I now prefer another type of person; one who is considerate, understanding of others, careful not to break down another person's self-respect.

" . . . My preferred person today is one who is always aware of the needs of others, or their pain and fear and unhappiness, and their search for self-respect. . . . I once liked clever people. Now I like good people."

The Lord commanded, "Cease to speak evil one of another." (D&C 136:23.) Gossiping and backbiting are two more foes of love. Kids often chant, "Sticks and stones can break my bones, but words can never hurt me." How wrong they are! The real truth is that hard words thrown can never be recovered.

In one neighborhood there used to be a little walking (and talking) group. As the group rounded the corner past a neighbor's house, one woman made a critical remark containing some bit of gossip she had recently heard about this neighbor. Her friend immediately listed several positive qualities about the same person, ending with, "I really like him!" The first woman had chosen to stab a person in the back. Her friend had effectively pulled out the knife and put it back in her hand, showing that a person can and should stick up for her friends.

Akin to backbiting and gossiping is the greatest all-time killer of loving relationships. See if you can recognize it in the following little example:

"You will never believe what I just heard about Mary!" Jane says, and then whispers her hot secret.

Her friend giggles at the news. "Whoever told you such a thing?"

"Well, Mary did, of course. But I promised I wouldn't tell a soul, so don't *you* say a word!"

Oh, the stories we could tell about broken confidences causing hurt feelings and destroying friendships! But we can sum it up all up in one sentence: If you don't want a secret to leak, *don't speak!*

Judging and prejudging other people are foes of love. There are times when we need to take a friend aside and quietly discuss a conflict or problem for that person's own good and growth. But wantonly passing judgments on people, flinging them out for the whole world to see and hear, does not build or lift. It often destroys. Remember the words of Mormon: "And now, my brethren, seeing that ye know the light by which ye may judge, which light is the light of Christ, see that ye do not judge wrongfully; for with that same judgment which ye judge ye shall also be judged." (Moroni 7:18.)

On the other hand, we do not know of anyone who has suffered from positive feedback. A person will glow inside when someone is kind enough to tell her she has performed well. Make it a point to observe good things about people, and when you do observe the good, tell the person so immediately. Don't ever let an opportunity pass to build up someone.

Contention can also destroy love. It is an old problem in the Church. The Lord said, "My disciples, in days of old, sought occasion against one another and forgave not one another in their hearts; and for this evil they were afflicted and sorely chastened." (D&C 64:8.) Bickering and strife still divide the Lord's disciples today.

We need to realize that many contentions originate within our own thoughts. The Lord asks, "And why beholdest thou the mote [speck of dust] that is in thy brother's eye, but considerest not the beam [large piece of timber] that is in thine own eye?" (3 Nephi 14:3.) We cannot change other people, but we have been given the free agency to examine ourselves and change our own behaviors and attitudes. As we do this, we will come closer to our goal of perfection.

If you are sure that the cause of the contention does not lie within yourself, try discussing it *privately with the people involved.* When you choose to take the problem elsewhere, words can slip and rumors can fly away on swift wings. If you cannot come to an agreement, possibly you can agree to disagree. Not every problem can be resolved, but you can go on loving anyway.

Remember, no matter what happens, the Lord requires that we forgive all men and warns that we cannot expect his forgiveness of our sins unless we forgive others. Unresolvable conflicts must be left in the Lord's hands. The Lord instructs us "to say in your hearts — let God judge between me and thee, and reward thee according to thy deeds." (D&C 64:11.)

Sarcasm, put-downs, negative teasing and joking, backbiting, gossiping, not keeping confidences, judging, and contention are all against our nurturing nature. So why do we allow them? Why aren't we more kind and generous to each other? Sometimes it is because of carelessness or lack of understanding, sometimes it is because of fear or distrust, and sometimes we are just plain envious or jealous.

Jealousy and its near-kinsman envy have numerous faces — all of them hideous. They are bitter, invidious feelings that can slither past our best spiritual guards to send messages of misery to our minds.

Experts cannot agree on a clear dividing line between jealousy and envy. For the purpose of this chapter, let's define jealousy as an emotion directed to people about people, and envy as an emotion directed to people about things, such as personal possessions, status, honors, abilities and talents, church positions, and so on.

What causes jealousy? After pulling book after book off the library shelves, and reading the theories of well-known psychologists, psychiatrists, medical doctors, and professional writers, we decided to return to the best authority of them all — the scriptures. In very plain language, Mormon answered this question: "Wherefore, all things which are good cometh of God; and that which is evil cometh of the devil; for the devil is an enemy unto God, and fighteth against him continually, and inviteth and enticeth to sin, and to do that which is evil continually." (Moroni 7:12.)

Teamed together, jealousy and envy are two of Satan's most powerful tools. When the Lord called Cain to account for killing his brother Abel, Cain whimpered, "Satan tempted me because of my brother's flocks [envy at its worst]. And I was wroth also; for his offering thou didst accept and not mine [or, 'you love Abel more than you love me,' a jealous reaction]." (Moses 5:38.)

In the Bible we read that "Israel loved Joseph more than all his children, because he was the son of his old age: and he made him a coat of many colours. And when his brethren saw that their father loved him more than all his brethren [note that it was not the beautiful coat that irked them, but the favoritism of their father], they hated him, and could not speak peaceably unto him [jealousy].

"And Joseph dreamed a dream, . . . and told it his brethren, and said . . . behold, the sun and the moon and the eleven stars made obeisance to me. . . . And his brethren envied him [or envied the power and position that they were afraid Joseph might obtain over them]." (Genesis 37:3-11.)

Motivated by envy and jealousy, Cain killed his brother Abel, and Joseph's brothers sold him for twenty pieces of silver to the Ishmeelites, who transported him to Egypt. Is it any wonder that Paul preached, "Now the works of the flesh are manifest, which are these; . . . Envyings, murders, drunkenness, revellings, and such like: of the which I tell you before, as I have also told you in time past, that they which do such things shall not inherit the kingdom of God." (Galatians 5:19, 21.) Mormon, writing to the latter-day Gentiles, commanded, "Turn, all ye Gentiles, from your wicked ways; and repent of your . . . envyings, and your strifes." (3 Nephi 30:2.) And the Lord has commanded, "strip yourselves of jealousies." (D&C 67:10.)

How do we overcome feelings of jealousy and envy? How do we rid ourselves of these mortal tendencies that destroy love? First, we must recognize the problem. In the article "The Hardest Truth I Ever Faced," one brave sister confessed, "For a long time I had been harboring feelings of resentment toward some of my relatives, without understanding why. Then one morning as I lay quietly in bed . . . the Spirit spoke and I heard words I didn't want to hear: 'You're jealous.'

"At first I resisted the thought. How could I be jealous of the people I had criticized? How could one who thought jealousy was wrong be jealous? But even as I protested, I knew it was true. And perhaps the truth would at last free me of my bad feelings." (Taken from the *Ensign*, August 1980, pp. 46-47.)

Next, we must take ownership of our problem. One of the hardest things for us, as humans, to do is to take responsibility for our weaknesses. We want to blame somebody else—anybody else! But we must recognize that the problem lies within ourselves before we can begin to correct it.

Then we can take the problem to the Lord. Moroni 7:45 gives a definition of charity that makes a good measuring stick. In every conflict we should ask ourselves, "Am I being long suffering and kind? Do I have feelings of envy or am I puffed up and proud? Have I been easily provoked? Do I rejoice in the iniquity or the sins and shortcomings of others? Am I bearing all these things well, keeping my hope bright, and enduring to the end?" If we answer no to any of those questions, it is time to get down on our knees and "pray unto the Father with all the energy of heart, that [we] may be filled with this love." (Moroni 7:48.)

A sister talks about her battle with negative feelings:

> One dark night I lay in bed, feeling weighed down with my own weaknesses. I stared out at the blackness that surrounded me; it was as dark as my own inner thoughts. I prayed for peace, for help, and for comfort. Very suddenly the blackness began to lift, replaced by a warmth that surrounded and penetrated my whole being: this, I knew immediately, was love—an incredible love! Fearing that the feeling would leave, I held my breath. The thoughts that tortured me fled before the light and I understood that even though I was weak and filled with shortcomings, my Heavenly Father loved me!

Our Heavenly Father loves each one of us in a way that is far beyond our comprehension. With his divine help, we can conquer jealousy, envy, or any of our other weaknesses — and win!

Armed with this knowledge of the power of prayer and the love of our Heavenly Father, we are ready to march into battle. The war with Satan is very real; he seeks to destroy us. By learning to recognize and wield the proper weapons, we can win. President Heber J. Grant was fond of telling this story:

> I believe there is a great deal in the story that some of you may have read, in which a donation was requested, and a man decided to give a ham.
>
> He had a smoke-house full of hams, and he had decided to give a ham to some poor person that needed a donation. When he went in there, he picked out a nice large ham, and the spirit came over him:
>
> "Now, that is a big ham; you don't need to give that person such a large ham; give him a little one."
>
> He said, "Shut up, Mr. Devil, or I will give him two hams," so he had no more trouble — none whatever. (*Gospel Standards*, Salt Lake City: Deseret Book Company, 1976, p. 283.)

In other words, we can effectively fight Satan's evil by counterattacking with double the goodness. Satan may whine, "Walk away. Turn down all invitations. Don't pick up the phone. Sever your relationship. It will be so much easier if you don't have to face the envy or jealousy. It hurts too much."

Why would Satan want you to do that? Because if you refuse to deal with the problem, you cannot conquer it; therefore, you will not grow. If Satan wishes you to walk away, then invest more time, be more available, serve with love. Instead of running away, try talking about your feelings with the person you are struggling with. This is difficult, but it is worth a try. Explain what is hurting you. Don't place the blame or lash out at the other person; instead, admit that you are jealous or envious and ask for understanding and patience.

Learn how to forgive and to be forgiven. When jealousy and envy enter a friendship, there is going to be pain. Many marriages and other relationships are destroyed because people cannot choke down their pride and say "I am sorry," or "I forgive you," or "Will you forgive me?" President Gordon B. Hinckley said, "I should like to say a word concerning charity of a different kind. I speak of charity in the sense of forgiveness, of tolerance of the failings of another, of the smothering of the feelings of jealousy and unkindness toward associates. . . . If there be any within the sound of my voice who have harbored grudges, who have let hatred develop in their hearts one toward another, I ask you to make the effort to turn around. Hatred always fails and bitterness always destroys, but 'charity never faileth.' (1 Cor. 13:8.)" (Taken from the Ensign, November 1981, p. 97.)

Satan may murmur, "See what she has? It is better than what you have, so tear down, criticize, demean, belittle, ridicule. Somebody needs to keep her humble." The best defense against such an attack is a direct counterattack: build up, praise, and encourage; moreover, learn to enjoy, to value, and to treasure the gifts, accomplishments, talents, even the possessions of your friends. The first time Jill heard Lauren sing she thought, somewhat enviously, Oh, to have a voice like Lauren's. That would be a wonderful gift. And so she once said to Lauren, "I would give my eyeteeth for your voice."

"Really? " Lauren said. "And what would you be willing to give me in exchange for my voice? Would you give me your writing talent or your ability for public speaking?"

"No! I need those talents."

Lauren smiled. "Oh, I see — you want my talent and all of your talents also. That's not fair!"

Lauren was right — and when Jill realized it, she stopped envying Lauren's talent and started to enjoy it. Once we get over envying our friends' abilities and talents we can benefit from them.

48

Satan may growl, "Two is company, but three is a crowd." It's easy to be envious of the good times our friends have with others. Satan would encourage exclusivity and cliquishness in our relationships. But the Lord never intended for all of our needs to be met by one or even two people. You will find that each person who enters your circle of love will bring you something new, beautiful, and unique. Some may be easy to talk with; some may need a listening ear; some will be blessed with many talents; some will have great spiritual gifts; some will be available to exchange services, like baby-sitting; some will be a joy just to socialize with, and so on.

As you reach out, your circle will expand and you will grow. Don't you want the same for others? If you do not, scrutinize your motives carefully. Someone once said, "In jealousy there is more self love than love." Jealousy and envy seek to possess, to claim territorial rights, to set boundaries. Love offers free agency.

Satan may snivel, "You cannot conquer jealousy or envy. They are overpowering and you are weak." Then he will probably try one of his favorite ploys, "You are discouraged, discouraged, discouraged."

Don't believe it. Start by setting some little goals. By achieving each little goal you will move ahead and eventually reach your destination. You will have some failures. When you do, congratulate yourself, since only people who are sincerely trying can fail. In Jill's house, when one of her family members auditions for a part in a play, a choir, a place in the talent show, or campaigns for a school office, whether the person makes it or not, the family throws a party. It takes courage to try, and courage should be celebrated.

Don't let Satan trap you into feeling as if you are a total failure because you failed to achieve one goal. Many times, one setback will cause a person to reflect on all the other mistakes in her life. These negative thoughts can become overwhelming, and discouragement breaks through. If you must turn your head to the past, look behind you and see how far you have traveled.

Conquering jealousy and envy will not be easy; however, battle by battle you will win the war. Our Heavenly Father placed us here on earth to succeed, not to fail. And with his help, as we struggle, we will gain strength. Through his servant Moroni, the Lord promised, "And if men come unto me I will show unto them their weakness. I give unto men weakness that they may be humble; and my grace is sufficient for all men that humble themselves before me; for if they humble themselves before me, and have faith in me, *then I will make weak things become strong unto them.*" (Ether 12:27; italics added.)

By stripping away jealousy, envy, and the other foes of love, we can create a happier life for ourselves and all those around us. We can tap that great power to build, lift, and nurture that is part of our divine inheritance.

We are told that after Christ's mission on the American continent, "There was no contention in the land, because of the love of God which did dwell in the hearts of the people. And there were no envyings, nor strifes, nor tumults . . . and surely there could not be a happier people among all the people who had been created by the hand of God." (4 Nephi 1:15-16.)

Someday this whole earth will be cleansed, and then it will be that way again, but we don't have to wait for the Millennium. We can each do our part by cleansing our inward vessels first (see Alma 60:23) and then reaching out to strengthen others.

CHAPTER   6

A Wall of Fears

All of us struggle with fears. Imagine each of these fears forming a block, and each of those blocks becoming part of a wall. Some people think that this wall protects them from the difficult world outside. It doesn't. Each of us is here to be tried and tested — no wall can help us avoid that. What this wall of fears does is to keep us from seeing the needs of our spirit brothers and sisters, and to obscure their ability to see our needs. It also stops us from developing close, loving relationships.

In an epistle written to his beloved son Moroni, Mormon taught that "perfect love casteth out all fear." (Moroni 8:16.) Then Mormon charted the way in which to obtain perfect love: "And the first fruits of repentance is baptism; and baptism cometh by faith unto the fulfilling the commandments; and the fulfilling the commandments bringeth remission of sins; and the remission of sins bringeth meekness, and lowliness of heart; and because of meekness and lowliness of heart cometh the visitation of the Holy Ghost, which Comforter filleth with hope and perfect love, which love endureth by diligence unto prayer, until the end shall come, when all the saints shall dwell with God." (Moroni 8:25-26.)

The wonderful first principles and ordinances of the gospel — faith, repentance, baptism, and receiving the gift of the Holy Ghost — are the beginning steps to perfect love, the only love that can remove fear. Next, we must be humble and seek perfect love by diligence in prayer. *Diligence* implies not one, but many prayers. Each and every time we find ourselves in a situation that is fearful, or in which we show anything less than pure love, we need to "pray unto the Father with all the energy of heart, that ye may be filled with this love, which he hath bestowed upon all who are true followers of his Son, Jesus Christ." (Moroni 7:48).

Strengthened with the bonds of love, you can boldly step out from behind your wall of fears, indeed, you may even find that you are excited about it! You are the one who must make the move; you cannot expect anyone to come flying over or crashing through your wall. The wise King Solomon said, "A man that hath friends must shew himself friendly." (Proverbs 18:24.)

Sir Isaac Newton said, "Men build too many walls and not enough bridges." Let us share with you some ways to pull down your wall, sometimes using those same blocks of fear to make a bridge to love.

Block 1: I'm not good enough

We are often shy about reaching out to others because we feel inadequate. We see all that they accomplish and feel that we just aren't good enough to be their friends.

This kind of feeling can be likened to a ride on an escalator. When you step onto an escalator, there are people above you and people below you, but there is very little room for anyone to stand right next to you. Similarly, we tend to feel that there are people who are better than we are. And, though we would be ashamed to admit it, most of us feel that there are people who are not quite as good as we are. (None of us would really place ourselves at the bottom of the heap, would we?)

We need to change our attitude and view our trip through life as a giant elevator in which we can all go up together. Then we can truly rejoice in each other's accomplishments and benefit from each other's talents.

Sometimes we feel inferior over things that are imagined, sometimes over things that are very real, but Eleanor Roosevelt concluded, "No one can make you feel inferior without your consent." Do you remember anything about Eleanor Roosevelt? You would think campaigning for her husband, Franklin D. Roosevelt, and serving as First Lady for more than twelve years would have been enough—but it wasn't! She served as a delegate to the United Nations General Assembly, was elected chairman of the UN's Human Rights Commission, helped draft the Universal Declaration of Human Rights, worked with the underprivileged, fought for equal rights for minorities, and wrote several books. She also had terrible buck teeth, which she obviously didn't sit around sulking about and feeling inferior over.

You are a child of our Heavenly Father and oh, how he loves you! He doesn't care if you are bald or short or never learned to play the piano. He pays no attention to whether your clothes or your house or your furniture or your cars cost as much as the neighbors'. He loves you! And our Savior pleads with each of us to "remember the worth of souls is great in the sight of God." (D&C 18:10.) This includes your soul! Don't let the "I'm not good enough" block of fear rule your life. You may miss out on some wonderful experiences.

Block 2: I don't fit in

Most of us have felt, at some time in our lives, as if we just didn't fit in. We tend to see people as fitting into certain specified groups. We think it is just easier to associate with people who are our age, or our color, or our religion, or our occupation, or our weight, or our financial status. We spend a lot of energy in seeking out our "group," and if we are a little uncomfortable we tell ourselves that we don't fit in. Many times this is a great excuse for not trying.

Lauren shares the worries she once felt about fitting in in a new neighborhood:

> When my husband and I were looking for a
> home to buy, the real estate agent showed us a cute
> rambler on a quiet cul-de-sac. One afternoon the
> real estate agent was driving me over to see the
> house for a second time. As luck would have it, we

stopped behind the school bus that was letting off some of the elementary school kids who lived in that neighborhood. I was astounded at the number of children who jumped through the yellow doors and onto the street; it was as if an entire colony of ants had gotten loose. We waited in the car for what seemed like ten minutes until all of the children were off the bus and walking toward their homes. Later, I learned that the stop was only the first of three in my new neighborhood.

Something inside of me screamed, "Every other family in the neighborhood has children and you don't have any. *You don't fit in!*"

It took me a long time to quiet that fear and understand that it didn't matter. Not one person ever mentioned the fact that we were the only ones who didn't have children and no one ever came up to me and said, "You don't fit in." In fact, many people were envious of my position because of the time I was able to spend with my husband. In their eyes we were free.

Once, when a friend came to visit, she exclaimed, "Listen to that!"

I listened. "I can't hear anything."

She rested her head on the back of the couch. "I know. Isn't it wonderful! It is so quiet here." My friend has a large family and she thought my home was heavenly.

We can learn a lot from people who are not in our "group." I learned so much from my friends who have children that I really felt better prepared when motherhood finally came. Besides, seeing some of my friends' struggles with their children helped take the hurt out of having to wait so long.

Sometimes block number two creeps up on people as they attend church meetings. In a church centered around the celestial

54

family, childless couples, single adults, wives or husbands with inactive or nonmember spouses, wonderful parents whose children have gone astray, and others who do not have strong marriages with happy children may feel that they do not fit. Also, newly baptized members, members who have recently moved into a ward or branch, or members returning to church after a period of inactivity may feel uneasy, wondering where their place is or even if there is a place for them.

Did you notice how large this list of people is? You may find that more than half of the people in your ward or branch belong in one of these categories. If you want to feel as if you really belong, then go out of your way to make others feel as if they really fit. Because they do! If you set a goal never to let another sister sit alone in a church meeting, you will never sit alone either. If you set a goal to cross the room and introduce yourself to at least one person each week, someone will always know your name. If you set a goal to talk to at least one person in between meetings, someone who really may need a friend, you will soon have many friends.

In one ward two large families moved in the same week onto the same street. As soon as the first family had unpacked the pans, they took dinner over to the second family. "We know how much it means to have support when you are moving in," the mother of the first family said. These two families immediately felt that they fit in: the first because they gave freely, the second because they received graciously.

President Gordon B. Hinckley said, "It is a wonderful time to be a member of the Church, with millions of members all belonging to the greatest community of friends in all the world. Wherever one goes as a faithful Latter-day Saint he will have instant friends if he makes his identity known." The reality is that you already belong. You already fit! Now it is up to you make yourself feel that way.

Block 3: She won't like me/She doesn't like me

Most of us have feelings of insecurity in our relationships. We worry that others won't like us. One sister expressed her struggle with these feelings:

I once thought that if someone really got to know me, if someone could really see what was in my heart, if a person had the ability to read my soul, they would immediately turn away and want nothing to do with me.

Some time ago there was a very talented, en-thusiastic, fun-loving woman in my ward and I really wanted to be her friend. But the "she won't like me" feeling prevented me from reaching out to her.

One evening we just started talking. Do you know what I found out? She really wanted to get to know me better and to be my friend, *but* she was afraid that if I really got to know her, if I really found out what she was like on the inside, I wouldn't like her. I was shocked! She had jumped into the icy waters of deep communication and I wasn't going to let her stay in there by herself, so I told her about my feelings. Expressing those fears helped both of us overcome them and, through this common bond, a friendship flourished.

In the following days and weeks I found out that my friend had many heartaches and tragedies in her life. It helped her to know that I wouldn't laugh or be insensitive when she revealed inner thoughts and feelings, and I felt better knowing that I could also share with her and not be ridiculed or turned away. Best of all, we found out that we liked each other!

Don't stop a relationship before it starts just because you *think* a person won't like you. Give yourself a chance. Give your potential friend a chance.

The "She won't like me" block is usually fixed with a strong mortar to the "She doesn't like me" block. You get past that first fear and timidly reach out, but unfortunately, your new friend responds with lukewarm aloofness. If your wall includes this block your immediate response is, "See, I was right. She doesn't like me!"

In your search for close, loving relationships you will find that other people are also facing many challenges. You may choose to befriend a person who does not know how to return offered love, or who is deeply involved with personal problems, or who really does not have much time, or who does not value your friendship as much as you value hers, or who is also hiding behind a wall of fears. Such a person will give as much as she is able to. Try not to interpret her inability to meet your expectations as "she doesn't like me" when, in fact, she probably hasn't made that judgment at all. The only thing that has really happened in such a situation is that the person you have reached out to has not responded in the way you wanted.

Ideally every person should return equally that which is given to them; however, that practically never happens. If you really value a friendship you may have to make all the phone calls, plan all the luncheon dates, and always be the one to offer or ask for help. In other words, you must give without thought of what you are going to get in return. This is part of unconditional love.

You may also have to step back and give the friendship room to grow. If you have ever planted carrots or radishes too close to each other you know that if they are crowded they do not develop fully. They are scrawny! Sometimes a person can feel crowded by an overanxious friend, and the only way to help friendship survive is to give it a little more space. Remember that "charity suffereth long, and is kind." (Moroni 7:45.) You may have to be the sole nurturer of a friendship for months or even years before it will blossom. Don't cut a friendship off at the roots because of the "She doesn't like me" block of fear. Recognize that you are once more fighting with your own insecurities.

Block 4: I might get hurt

In every relationship where there is caring or love, there is also an element of risk. People can hurt each other to the same depth, degree, and intensity that they love each other. Lehi taught, "For it must needs be, that there is an opposition in all things." (2 Nephi 2:11.)

This principle is illustrated clearly in parenthood. There is no greater love than that between a parent and a child. Who can bring you more joy than your children? Who, also, can bring you more sorrow than your children? The same is true of any people who care deeply for each other: they can, and sometimes do, hurt each other deeply.

The "I might get hurt" block is a whole wall in itself to many people. We live in a society that is frightened of pain. If we have a headache, we take an aspirin. There are medicines for stomachaches, backaches, toothaches, earaches, and even placebo pills for imagined aches. But there just isn't an easy remedy for a heartache and perhaps that is why we fear it so much.

Yet, it obviously is not in our Heavenly Father's plan for true followers of Christ to insulate themselves from pain. The Lord commanded, "Love your enemies, bless them that curse you, do good to them that hate you, and pray for them which despitefully use you, and persecute you." (Matthew 5:44.) This is hardly a prescription for pain-free relationships. The question is, how can we ever gain the maturity to love our enemies, if we are so fearful of being hurt that we cannot give complete and full love to our friends?

When we experience deep emotional pain inflicted by another person, it is natural to want to pull back—like jerking a hand off a hot stove—taking the pain and the hurt with us. "I'll never trust anyone again," we sometimes feel. But trust is one of the vital organs of a loving relationship. Without it the relationship will shrink away and eventually die. Forgiveness heals deep emotional wounds, bringing peace and restoring trust. If a hurt is allowed to go unforgiven, it will poison the relationship and the unforgiving person as well. It is only through total forgiveness and renewed trust that we can let go of the hurt and extend our hand again. Forgiveness brings great joy and peace, crushing the "I might get hurt" block.

We have talked about removing fears through love, forgiveness, and trust. To these things we would like to add the important quality of faith. Marvin J. Ashton promised, "Fear in our lives can be conquered if we will but have faith and move forward with purpose."

The Apostle Peter showed courage and faith many times. On one such occasion, the winds were howling and the ship he was in was being tossed about in the waves. Then the disciples saw Jesus walking on the water. Peter didn't wait for the Savior to come to him, but called out, "Lord, if it be thou, bid me come unto thee on the water." In a similar fashion, we can't wait for others to come around our wall of fears; we have to be willing to walk out from behind it.

Jesus beckoned Peter to come. Jesus knew what terror the water would hold for Peter, but he also knew that Peter would not grow spiritually if he stayed safely in the boat, just as we cannot grow spiritually if we stay safely behind our walls. Then, with faith, Peter jumped out of the boat and started walking on the water! Many times we don't give Peter enough credit for trying, focusing instead on his failure. Peter could have said, "Never mind. It looks pretty scary out there. I'll stay here in the boat and wait until things get a little calmer." But he didn't.

The scriptures say that when Peter "saw the wind boisterous, he was afraid." When you reach out, you are going to face strong winds of adversity. Satan is not going to overlook the fact that you can do much good if you get over your fears. He is going to stir up a storm. With his strong opposition, your fears may return. You may even doubt and, like Peter, begin to sink. But remember that Peter cried out, "Lord, save me. And immediately Jesus stretched forth his hand, and caught him." Just as Jesus did not let Peter fall, neither will he let you fall! However, as our Lord takes you gently by the hand and lifts you up, be prepared for a brotherly scolding just as he gave to Peter: "O thou of little faith, wherefore didst thou doubt?" (Matthew 14:24-31.) The Lord chastens those he loves. (See D&C 95:1.)

Peter continued to fight with his fears and doubts. It was fear that caused him to deny the Christ three times outside the doors of the palace of the high priest while the Savior was being unlawfully tried inside. But Peter never gave up. He moved forward with faith and purpose, eventually conquering his fears and becoming the chief apostle of his day. Our Heavenly Father is mindful of the righteous desires of your heart and he will help you achieve them.

Pulling down the wall that has hidden and protected you for many years may be a very frightening experience in itself. It takes time and patience, but the risks you take and the pain you might experience from removing blocks of fear from your life will be worth it!

CHAPTER 7

Communicating Love

People who wish to encircle others with love consistently send out messages of love. They do it by the way they greet people, smile, touch others with a handshake or hug, remember names, listen, involve others in their lives, and express their feelings. They know how to communicate love sincerely. The ability to communicate is a skill that must be learned. This chapter will help you acquire this knowledge so you can more effectively reach out to others.

Greet with a smile

Start by greeting everyone with a smile. Smiling is a talent that anyone can acquire; with practice, you can even become a grand master smiler. Think of it: no matter how many long hours of practice you put in on the piano, you may never play in a concert. No matter how many voice lessons you take, you might not get the lead in an opera. But your smile can be the star of the show every day.

First, practice in front of every mirror you come across. When you brush your teeth, comb your hair, or put on makeup, practice your biggest, broadest grin. One of our friends practiced when she stopped at red lights. She stretched her chin up until she could see her mouth in the rearview mirror and then tried out her grin. She tried large, toothy grins, closed-mouth grins, and even demure half smiles. She got some strange looks from other drivers and passengers, but now when she walks into a room the sunshine seems to follow her.

Don't worry if your teeth are spaced unevenly or yellowed or crooked or your smile is lopsided. People who are self-conscious about their smiles often cover them up with a hand. Don't do it! Let your smile shine through.

Next, practice your smile with your friends and family. If they are not used to seeing your lips curved up they may ask, "Are you okay?" But soon they will get accustomed to it, and then, when you are not smiling, they will ask, "Are you okay?"

When you have mastered that, smile at strangers. During the back-to-school shopping crush a young store clerk was running in and out of the stock room, trying to retrieve merchandise for a customer. The customer grumbled at each item the clerk showed him and finally stomped off without making a purchase. The clerk return to the cash register, silent and sullen.

Another customer commented, "Sometimes it can be pretty rough working for the public, can't it?"

The clerk looked up and saw a sympathetic smile. "Sometimes, but most of the time people are pretty nice," she replied, returning the smile. As the second customer turned to leave she noticed that the clerk had a smile for the customer behind her and that smile was also returned. A smile is a gift that you can give to anyone around you.

The power of touch

Have you ever noticed how often Christ extended his hands and touched those around him to heal, to bless, and to ordain? When a leper came to him and asked to be cleansed, "Jesus put forth his hand, and touched him, saying, I will; be thou clean." (Matthew 8:3.) When he found Peter's mother-in-law sick with a fever "he touched her hand, and the fever left her." (Matthew 8:15.) When two blind men came to Jesus begging, "Thou Son of David, have mercy on us," Jesus asked them, "Believe ye that I am able to do this? They said unto him, Yea, Lord. Then touched he their eyes, saying, According to your faith be it unto you." (Matthew 9:28-29.)

In the Book of Mormon we read that Jesus "took their little children, one by one, and blessed them, and prayed unto the Father for them." (3 Nephi 17:21.) Can you picture Christ surrounded by infants, toddlers, and older children? He reaches forth his hand, marked by the wound of the nail, and gently takes the hand of a little girl in the circle. He smiles and lifts the little one onto his lap and places his hands on her small head. After blessing all the children his joy was so great that he wept. (3 Nephi 17:22.)

Human touch is important, both eternally and temporally. One of the first things we learn in mortality is that close bodily contact brings forth feelings of safety, warmth, and love. A baby quiets when cuddled and rocked. A small child climbs on Mother's lap. Older children lean against their parents or brothers and sisters in church or during story time. Hugging, tickling, gentle pinching and poking, back rubbing, tousling the hair, and wrestling are common ways in which families make that human connection.

But sometime, somehow an invisible box called "personal space" closes in around each of us. When someone sits or stands too close to us, we automatically slide or back away until we are at a comfortable distance. The amount of personal space we need varies with each person and between people. Think of the differences in the amount of room you need to feel comfortable when you are sitting by (1) your spouse, boyfriend, or fiancé, (2) a friend, (3) a stranger, or (4) someone you have negative feelings toward. You probably don't need much personal space at all with the first, and yet you may not feel comfortable being in the same building with a person you have had a confrontation with.

We need to respect people's need for personal space, but there are ways we can quickly pop in and out of that space, creating warm stirrings of love and friendship. One of these "safe" times is with a handshake.

Let's forget all the traditional rules of etiquette between men and women and concentrate on this important communication of love. Have you ever extended your hand to someone, only to be kept waiting there with your hand dangling in midair? Even a few seconds of hesitation from the other person can feel like minutes. During that time the negative messages begin to flow: What have I done to him? Why am I being rejected? Is he mad at me? In reality the other person's hand is probably just sweaty or cold and clammy, and he hesitates out of embarrassment. Unfortunately, in those seconds of hesitation a negative message is communicated: "unfriendly!"

When a hand is extended, reach back immediately! Don't squish like a juicer — that maims ring-decorated pinkies. Neither do you want to let your hand rest gently and corpselike in the palm of another during a handshake. The right grip is actually a natural reflex. Have you ever pressed your finger into the hand of a newborn baby? The tiny fingers close firmly and gently. What a wonderful, secure feeling that is! When the grip is just right, don't pump or saw — just move the hand slightly up and down. An added positive gesture is to place the second hand on top of the two clutched hands. And, of course, look the person in the eyes and *smile!*

Hugging is another way that we can reach through the personal space that surrounds most of us and communicate friendship and love. A single mother stood before her sisters in a Relief Society meeting and, with tears in her eyes, spoke of her struggles in raising her small family without the aid and companionship of a husband. Then she said, "One thing that has really helped me is the warm hugs I receive from my friends. I can be having the worst day and a friend will come up and say, 'You look like you need a hug' and then give me a warm squeeze. It is always perfect timing and it always makes me feel better."

For some people, a hug is uncomfortable. But we believe that people need to be touched whether they know it or not. If you feel that someone is uncomfortable with a hug, you might simply touch a hand or an elbow. In this way you can still communicate your love and friendship without making the person uneasy.

Remember names

There are no dearer sounding words in all of speech than a person's own name. Remembering (or forgetting) a name or mispronouncing a name is also a loud and clear communication of friendship or the lack thereof.

Jill likes to tell of one special person's talent for remembering and using her name:

> When I was working for a local TV studio I often had the opportunity to meet famous people who came in to be interviewed on the air. It was in this way I met Gordon Jump, star of *WKRP in Cincinnati*. After the show, I introduced myself to him and we chatted briefly. When I excused myself, he said very politely, "It was a pleasure meeting you, Mrs. Major." I was impressed that he had listened for my name and used it!
>
> About ten minutes later Mr. Jump left the studio, but he was still standing in the lobby when an important phone call came in for him. I volunteered to relay the message. "Mr. Jump, you have a phone call at the reception desk," I told him.
>
> He smiled at me. "Thank you, Jill," he answered.
>
> From our brief encounter I decided that Mr. Jump was really friendly and he cared about people. Why? Just because he remembered my name.

Remembering names is important; it communicates caring. It says, "You are an important person to me." If you are one of those people whose mind seems to have a trapdoor through which all names are released into some dark, dusty, forgotten room of the brain, don't despair. There is hope.

One of the biggest reasons most people do not remember a name is that they don't hear it in the first place. The introduction takes place; the name is mumbled; you didn't quite hear it, but you are too embarrassed to ask for the name to be repeated. If that happens, swallow a little pride and simply say, "I'm sorry. I didn't quite catch your name. Will you say it for me again?"

Sometimes we hear the name but quickly forget it because

we are distracted or we aren't concentrating. Learn to stop and focus in on people during introductions. Say the name over silently several times and then use it immediately. "It is really nice to meet you, Mr. Jones." Then use the name again before leaving that person.

There are several excellent memory books on the market that explain how to use word association to remember a name and its owner. If you really struggle with remembering names, borrow one of these books from the local library and put it to use. It is amazing how quickly you can train your mind to remember and retrieve names. It soon becomes a habit.

Just as important as remembering the name is pronouncing it correctly. It is just plain uncomfortable to hear your own name mispronounced, so during introductions pay close attention to correct pronunciations of other people's names.

Contributing to conversation

Many potentially wonderful friendships are never started because one or both of the people are nervous about starting a conversation and keeping it going. What do you say? Most people like to talk about themselves, so questions are an easy way to start a conversation. Questions that require simple yes or no answers are often roadblocks to conversation. Keep inquiries open-ended: Tell me about the place you used to live, or your job. What do you enjoy doing in your spare time? What did you do this morning?

Be careful to keep questions limited in scope. "Tell me about yourself" is like flinging open a dozen doors at one time. The person may just stand there, feeling confused, wondering which passageway to turn into.

Above all, don't be afraid to contribute to the conversation by sharing some of your own history, background, ideas, feelings, interests, and hobbies. When one person is asking all the questions and the other giving all the answers, it soon begins to feel like an interrogation instead of a friendly chat.

As important as knowing what to say is knowing what not to ask. The Church has an abundance of people who do not live in traditional family circumstances. The prophets' calls to collect and record family histories do not include the personal details of your neighbors' lives! It is not important for us know what happened in a divorce; how a spouse became inactive; why an older single adult has not married; why a couple has a very large family, a very small family, or no children; or about any other personal family traumas. Neither should we rain down judgments: "There must be something wrong with her if she is divorced," or "She isn't married because she is too picky." Nor should we make assumptions: "They probably waited to have children until after they finished school or they bought a home or because she wanted a career." We need to be sensitive to other people's feelings!

Instead of asking "Are you married?" or "How many children do you have?," try saying, "Tell me about your family." Then the person is free to talk about her brothers and sisters, her aunts and uncles, her genealogy back to Adam, or anything else that comes to mind.

No matter how delicate we try to be there are going to be times when, out of ignorance, we say inappropriate things. If this happens, put your arms around the person you have offended and immediately ask for forgiveness. The relationship will grow because your friends will learn to trust your efforts to be sensitive.

If you have been a recipient of this type of prying and grilling, our advice is: *refuse to be offended.* People do not mean to hurt your feelings. In fact, in most cases they have no idea their questions cause you any pain. You cannot control the words of others, but you can control how you react to them. Try to see that when a friend puts her foot in her mouth it is nasty-tasting and humiliating to her also.

Many people have left the Church because of the unthoughtfulness of others. What a shame! We have a friend who was once the victim of cruel deeds and harsh words, but his words were ever tender and merciful. He said, "Father, forgive them; for they know not what they do." (Luke 23:34.)

Listening more effectively

In order to listen to someone, first you must focus your attention on what that person is saying. While someone chats away, your mind may be chugging down several tracks. Perhaps there will be a pause in the conversation that jolts you back. You ask a question. "I just explained that to you," your friend says with exasperation in her voice. The conversation has just crashed. To hear, you must have a one-track mind, and it must be on the same track as your friend's.

Once you start hearing, then you can listen. The two have some of the same elements, but they are not the same action. Listening is deeper than hearing. Listening—not just passively tuning in, but actively listening—is the most important part of a conversation. It communicates love. When you listen, you are using your ears not only to process words, but also to interpret the tone of voice. You are using your eyes to see facial expressions, body movement, and responses. You separate yourself from your own life and from your own emotions at that time so that you can feel what the other person is going through.

For example, when you ask the traditional question, "How are you?" you will probably hear the conventional answer, "Fine." Now, if you took a survey on how many people are a plain, flat "fine" all the time, the numbers would probably be few. Now listen! You might hear that your friend's voice has a musical ring and see that there is a certain extra brightness in her eyes. Then, perhaps, you could say something like, "You look extra happy today. Did something special happen?" Or you may see that your friend's shoulders droop, and hear melancholy in her voice. In this case you could make a comment such as, "You look like you are feeling a little tired or a little down." People will be surprised and delighted that you genuinely care enough to really listen.

You don't have to be a psychologist to be a good listener— just use good old common sense. Suppose you are speaking about a sensitive, serious, personal subject and the person you are talking with reacts in one of the following ways: (1) He or she busily looks out the window or at the television. (2) He or she picks up a book or newspaper and begins thumbing through it. (3) He or she breaks into the middle of your sentence and doesn't let you complete it. (4) After you finish your thought, he or she quickly interjects, "I don't mean to change the subject,

68

but . . . , " which of course means, "I really mean to change the subject, so. . . . " How do you feel when one of these situations occurs? Well, if you feel put down, belittled, unimportant, and inconsequential, common sense tells you how other people feel under the same circumstances.

Notice that most of the words in the preceding sentence are negative. We need to build each other with positive feelings. A good listener can make another person feel important and worthwhile. When someone is talking to you, look into her eyes, not at her feet, her scarf, out the window, or at the newspaper. This is so basic that even small children know it. Many times a child will take both of her little hands, place them on each side of an adult's cheeks and physically turn the face so that he is looking right straight in her eyes. The message is very clear: "You are not listening to me unless you are looking at me."

Nod occasionally, and say "uh-huh." When appropriate, ask a simple question that shows you are interested in the topic. And even if the topic doesn't interest you, don't change the subject until there is a comfortable break in the conversation. Yes, this does take some patience and endurance, especially if the speaker likes to spend hours chattering on about her last fifteen operations, but the payoff is, that person feels important because you really listened! Don't get perturbed if you can't get a word in edgewise. Think of listening as a compassionate service, since it truly is. According to Marion D. Hanks, "Every human being is trying to say something to others, trying to cry out, 'I am alive. Notice me! Speak to me! LISTEN to me! Confirm for me that I am important, that I matter.' "

Finally, listen with a kind ear. One of our favorite quotations expresses this beautifully: "Oh, the comfort, the inexpressible comfort, of feeling safe with a person, having neither to weigh thoughts, nor measure words, but pouring them all right out just as they are — chaff and grain together — certain that a faithful hand will take and sift them, keep what is worth keeping and with the breath of kindness blow the rest away." The three of us often dump on each other, secure in the knowledge that the others will listen without making judgments or passing on negative thoughts and feelings. Oh, what a wonderful treasure is a friend who knows how to listen with a kind ear!

Don't be afraid to ask

Many people feel it is a show of weakness to have to ask for assistance. These same independent people are often those who enjoy serving most, yet, even in a personal crisis situation, they do not utter a word of request and they turn down all offers of help. It is a shame! Not only do they deny others the opportunity to serve them, but they also close many doors to strengthening bonds of love. When you ask a person to do something for you, you are paying her a compliment. You are saying, "I need help and I trust you enough to provide that help." If your heart is in the right place, you are also communicating the message, "I will be there anytime you need me." Later, when that person needs a favor, she will remember that you asked her, and so she will feel more comfortable asking you in return. So ask an acquaintance for that needed ride, for a cup of borrowed sugar, for help with your genealogy, for an hour of baby-sitting, to tape record an important meeting that you must miss, to sit by you in Relief Society because you are feeling a bit uneasy, to help you find just the right flowers for your garden, for advice on child raising, to bring in a meal when you are sick, and so on. That acquaintance will quickly become a friend.

Another type of asking is to ask a person to do something *with* you. This communicates the message, "I like your company. I want to be with you. I value your friendship." Many people do not ask because they fear being turned down or rejected. When a person is unavailable to do something with you, do not interpret this to mean, "I don't want to be your friend," when it probably means, "I don't like doing that" or "I am too busy that evening" or "I am very shy and uncomfortable." Even if you get turned down, you have communicated your desire to be a friend.

Say "I love you"

"I love you" is such a simple phrase, yet for many people these words are very difficult to say. A friend shared how the words "I love you" changed her life:

When I was growing up I never heard the words "I love you" used in my home. I knew that I was loved. My parents worked very hard to see that I received the things I needed and they tried to spend as much time as possible with me. Yet, these words were never said. For some reason they were embarrassing. Fortunately, I married a wonderful man who expresses his love to our children and me several times each day.

After being away nearly ten years from the home I grew up in, I began to feel a deep yearning to express my feelings of love to my brothers, sisters, Mom, and Dad. It was hard, but I set a goal for myself and then I made opportunities to do it. I remember walking Mom out to the car, keeping the conversation going, trying to find just the right moment. Finally, as Mom got ready to shut the door I took a deep breath and said, "Mom, I just want you to know that I really love you."

"I love you too," she said quietly, then we hugged. I stood on the driveway for a long time after my mother left, wiping away tears of joy, reliving that moment, wondering how something so simple could have taken me so long to do. I decided right then that each time I left a member of my family, they would know how I felt.

It still isn't easy, but I have noticed that a great miracle has taken place in my family. Now, those words that were never spoken are used by everyone.

In this chapter we have talked about many ways to communicate love. When you do one of these things, such as greeting someone with enthusiasm, it is like giving a person a beautiful helium balloon—what a great lift! If you learn to use many of these skills together—a smile, a firm handshake or a needed hug, remembering a person's name and pronouncing it correctly, a caring conversation—it is like presenting someone with a whole bouquet of beautiful, colorful balloons. But just as helium balloons float away if they are not anchored, these communications of love may drift away also, unless they are tied down securely with frequent verbal expressions of love. Learn to express your love and do it often. It will brighten cloudy eyes, turn up the corners of a downcast mouth, and scatter shadows of loneliness. When you communicate love, you will find that miracles will bloom all around you.

CHAPTER 8

Love Encircles Golden Friends

King Mosiah gave a strict command to be followed throughout all the churches in his kingdom that "there should be no persecutions among them, that there should be an equality among all men; that they should let no pride nor haughtiness disturb their peace; that every man should esteem his neighbor as himself." (Mosiah 27:3-4.) As true followers of Christ, we too should live by these words. There should not be any room for acts of inequality toward our neighbors. We should be free of the rumors that we, the Mormon people, are interested only in making proselytes, not in making friends. Yet, stories circulate of Mormon families who held their arms open in friendship until their nonmember or less-active neighbors showed no interest in the Church; then they folded their arms and bowed out of the friendship.

Part of the problem is that many of us, keeping the emphasis on missionary work in mind, tend to look at others first as golden contacts, so we become their friends. We need to reverse the order of priority and look at others first as golden friends. This does not mean that we do not share the gospel. We should give the best of our lives to those we love. But by placing the emphasis on the friendship first, we will never leave a friend stranded by the wayside.

Jesus taught the duties of being a neighbor in the parable of the good Samaritan. These duties have important parallels today.

The story begins with a man who traveled on the dangerous, dusty road that linked Jerusalem with Jericho. Thieves attacked the man, stole his clothes, and left him bloody, bruised, and half dead. Today, our less-active Mormon neighbors are often people who fell among bad company, usually in their teenage years. These robbers professed to be friends, but stripped the people of their beliefs, wounded them by introducing bad habits, and departed, leaving them half dead spiritually. Sometimes the robbers are Mormons who have set bad examples. Perhaps they stripped their neighbors of their right to be accepted members of the neighborhood, wounded them by ignoring them or doing things that the gospel expressly commands not to do, and departed, leaving them with bad feelings about all members of the Church.

Christ's parable continued with a priest and a Levite, both respected and important men in the Jewish church, who, seeing the poor man, crossed the road and walked on. Do we also at times get in a hurry, usually to attend to one of our many church duties, and so pass by those in our neighborhood who desperately need our love?

But then the Lord told about a Samaritan, one who traditionally was treated by Jews with bitterness, intolerance, and even hatred, because of religious differences. The Samaritan saw the poor man and felt compassion for him so he knelt down by the man's side and bound up his wounds (took in a plate of cookies, helped unload the moving van, assisted in unpacking), poured in oil and wine (smiled and waved, lent a listening ear), and set him on his own beast (opened the doors to his home, included him in parties and gatherings), and brought him to an inn and took care of him (brought in a meal when there was sickness in the family).

"And on the morrow when he departed, he took out two pence, and gave them to the host [involved other people in including and encouraging the new friend], and said unto him, Take care of him; and whatsoever thou spendest more, when I come again, I will repay thee." (Even though responsibilities of work, church, family, and community took him away, he returned to his non-Mormon or less-active Mormon friends.) (See Luke 10:30-37.)

Through this parable the Lord taught that anyone who needs our love, compassion, and help becomes our neighbor, whether that person lives near us or not. He also taught that a good neighbor would never leave another stranded by the wayside. Decide now that whether your nonmember friend decides to join the Church or not, or whether your less-active friend decides to become active or not, you will always stand by her and be her faithful friend!

Another complaint about Mormons is that they are cliquish or clannish. Yes, we do enjoy being with one another, and there is nothing wrong with that, but could we try harder to include those who do not attend our church activities every week? Could we expand our circle of friends and bring in those who do not believe the way we do? Sometimes we fail to do so because of fears that creep up; sometimes we get so involved in what we are doing that we don't take the time; sometimes we just don't know how to begin. But it is worth the effort to get over fears, take the time, and learn how to begin. Extending a hand to our nonmember and less-active member neighbors adds variety and great riches to life.

The experience of friendshipping a less-active member is a favorite memory for Lauren and Jill. When Susan and Lee moved into their ward, Lauren, Jill, and their husbands decided to make a conscious, consistent effort to be good neighbors and great friends. At the time, the fact that Susan and Lee smoked heavily seemed to be an obstacle. Where could they go that they could all be comfortable? Finally Jill came up with a brilliant idea: "How about a hockey game?" Lauren hesitated. She had never been to a hockey game and wasn't sure she ever wanted to go.

"It really would be the perfect place," Jill assured her. "We would be able to talk and be entertained at the same time. Besides, if either Susan or Lee want to smoke, they could just go out into the lobby for a few minutes."

The date was set and Susan and Lee were delighted to be invited. Susan was a hockey fan and had a basic understanding of the game, so whenever the others didn't understand why a player was penalized, they asked Susan. If Susan didn't know, she simply tapped the shoulder of the person sitting in front of her and asked him. One time, after receiving an explanation from a fan, Susan turned to them and said, "Hockey people are such friendly people!" That was probably true, but Susan was also friendly. She wasn't afraid to talk to strangers. In fact, from the first time that she met anyone, that person was Susan's friend.

After the hockey game Jill and Lauren invited Susan to a ladies-only evening at the opera *Madame Butterfly*. She accepted, but several days before the opera Jill got a phone call. "I'm sorry, but I won't be able to go with you," Susan said with disappointment in her voice.

"Is everything all right?" Jill asked.

"No. I'm in the hospital. The doctor says I have a blood clot in my lung." Susan sounded understandably frightened. "I was wondering if Ken could come and help my brother give me a blessing?" Jill and Lauren were excited to find out that Susan's family were active in the Church and that Susan had also been very active as a teenager.

Susan came home from the hospital a few days later with strict instructions from the doctor: *quit smoking!* During the next few weeks, while Susan was going through nicotine withdrawal, all her friends tried their best to help her. It seemed that each time Susan would feel the incredible urge to have a cigarette, to the point that she couldn't control it, Heavenly Father would gently nudge Ken, Jill, Bret, or Lauren. The prompting would come, "Call Susan" or "Visit Susan." They found out as they dropped by or picked up the phone that Susan desperately needed their support at that moment. It was a great lesson in learning to listen to the Spirit.

It was during those long weeks that the bishopric asked Jill to direct the roadshow. In protest Jill said, "But I've never directed anything!"

The bishop's counselor just grinned, "Great! Then you are qualified."

"Immediately, Jill called all of her friends for help, which, fortunately for her, is everyone in the ward. When Jill called Lauren she asked, "Would you please choreograph the road-show?"

"But I have never choreographed anything," she protested.

"Great! Then you are qualified," Jill answered gleefully.

One day Jill mentioned the road show to Susan. Susan was excited and wanted to know what she could do to help. Jill decided to let Susan assist Lauren with the choreography.

Susan and Lauren were discussing the road show one afternoon on the way home from a doctor visit. "I know Jill is directing and you are choreographing the road show, but what are Ken and Bret going to do?" Susan asked.

"I don't think they are going to do anything," Lauren replied.

"Well, you can just tell Ken and Bret that if I have to quit smoking, they can certainly be in the road show!" Susan said emphatically. The cast of characters for the road show was the "Fruit of the Bloom" family. Each person on stage dressed up as a giant fruit. There were apples, bananas, peaches, grapes, straw-berries, cherries, pears, oranges, and even fruit flies — the villains! A large kitchen with huge cabinets and a giant refrigerator formed the set. All of the fruity characters entered through the refrig-erator door. Ken, a distinguished administrative law judge, was a giant banana. Bret, a corporate controller, was a dancing pear. As Susan said, "Fair is fair."

When Susan and Lauren finished the blocking and all the dancers had learned their parts, Susan felt disappointed. She no longer had a responsibility, but she still wanted to be involved. Lauren then had a brilliant idea: the refrigerator needed a light! Someone found Susan a long, black, hooded cape and a large electrician's light. Each time the refrigerator door swung open, she held up the light and turned it on. Susan was so excited about her part that she invited her family to come and watch her perform. After the last performance she was given the "Light of the Road Show" award.

Susan, Jill, and Lauren became even closer friends over the next several months. One Saturday evening Jill received a phone call. "I was wondering what time Sunday School starts?" Susan asked.

Jill stammered momentarily, surprised at the question. "Ten A.M.," she finally said.

"Okay, we'll see you in the morning," Susan replied.

Jill hung up the phone, wondering why it had never occurred to her to ask Susan to come to church. At 9:55, Susan and Lee walked into church for the first time in twenty years.

Early one evening Susan called Jill with some bad news. Her voice was shaking as she said, "I've been to the doctor today. They told me I have cancer and they only give me six months to live."

Jill was stunned. "Susan, are you alone?" she asked.

"Yes," came the quiet reply.

"I'll be right over." Jill spent the next several hours with Susan, crying, talking, sharing, and eventually laughing.

The following weeks were filled with visits to doctors and radiation treatments at the hospital. This wasn't new to Susan; she had already had one bout with cancer a few years before. Susan was sick and stayed in bed most of the time during the duration of the treatments. Susan's mother, Claudia, came to live with the family and take care of their needs. When Claudia couldn't be there, Jill, Lauren, and other neighbors took turns fixing Susan breakfast in the morning and sitting on the edge of her bed in the afternoon, talking or playing games.

About that same time Clint DeYoung and John Draper, two teenagers in the neighborhood who had become acquainted with Susan through the road shows, brought her a dozen red roses. (Does this give you any idea how important it is to get our nonmember and less-active neighbors involved in activities where they can meet a lot of friends?) "These are the first roses I ever gave a girl," Clint told Susan. Almost every time anyone saw Susan after that she just glowed as she retold the story of the visit and the roses.

As the weeks dragged on, Susan became more and more ill and Jill and Lauren felt more frustrated and helpless. The cancer not only ate away at Susan physically, but it also devoured her hope and optimism. Her usual cheery nature began to darken. As Susan's birthday approached, Jill and Lauren hunted for something to lift her spirits.

"I know," Jill said. "Let's make her a Depression Emergency Kit!" They purchased some medicine bottles from the pharmacy and labeled them like prescriptions. Then they filled the bottles with various items, mostly things they found in their homes. Here is a list:

Take one when:

you are feeling under the weather
   (a miniature paper umbrella)
you have no pep (Pepto Bismol tablets)
you can't put it together (safety pins)
you can't bear it any longer (gummy bears)
there is no joy in your life (Almond Joy candy bar)
you are sick and tired of life (brown paper "barf" bag)
you are at the end of your rope (a small piece of rope)
you are feeling wiped out (baby wipes)
you are feeling blue (brightly colored crayons)
you really blew it (balloons)
you have no get up and go (a battery)

"Can you think of anything for 'when you need a lift'?" Jill asked.

Lauren began laughing out loud. "I think we should try to find a size 64 triple E bra!"

They found just what they were looking for at Deseret Industries: a huge, black, lacy treasure for only fifty cents. After a great deal of exertion they managed to stuff that bra into one of the prescription bottles. Then they wrapped up their kit and drove to Susan's house.

Susan was lying in bed, but when Jill and Lauren marched in singing "Happy Birthday" she managed a weak smile. Susan's mother joined them, and together they watched Susan open her gift. When she pulled off the wrapping paper and read "Depression Emergency Kit" on the decorated shoebox, she looked a bit puzzled. She lifted the lid and read what was printed on the inside: Dr. Major and Dr. Leifson. Office hours: anytime. Susan lifted each bottle out of the box and read the label. She was too weak to unscrew the lids, so Lauren sat by her side, unscrewed each lid, and set the cap on top so she could lift it off and look inside. As she opened each bottle, Susan's expressions slowly began to change. First, there was a faint smile, then a larger smile, then a small chuckle. Susan lifted out the last bottle and read the label out loud: "Take one when you need a lift." She handed the bottle to Lauren, who loosened the lid, being extra careful not to allow Susan to see what was inside. Susan lifted the lid, looked inside, looked up at Jill and Lauren, then back to the bottle. Jill and Lauren couldn't hold back the laughter. Just a little tug on the black cloth brought the entire bra popping out of the bottle and into her lap. Tears of laughter were rolling down all their faces as Susan held up her new gift by the straps for everyone to admire.

A few days later the doctors discovered a large tumor at the back of Susan's skull. Her family moved her to the hospital so that she could receive the care and the pain medication she needed to remain comfortable. Jill and Lauren stayed by her side as much as possible. One special, memorable visit they entered her hospital room and found Susan very groggy from medication. She opened her eyes slowly to see who was there and then raised up her hand toward them. "I don't feel much like talking," she whispered.

"That's all right," they replied. "We just dropped by to let you know we are thinking about you."

"Really? You came all this way just for that?" Susan asked.

Jill and Lauren both nodded their heads.

"My crazy friends," Susan said quietly as she squeezed both their hands.

Susan lived only two weeks after her birthday.

Jill and Lauren miss Susan and wish that they could have had more time with her. They are anxious to see Susan again and look forward to that glorious day when they can once again throw their arms around her and laugh and talk with her. And whether she accepts the gospel or not, Susan will always be their friend!

Friendshipping a nonmember may be a new experience for you, especially if you grew up surrounded by Mormon friends and family. Here are some suggestions on how to begin:

1. Visit your neighbor in her own surroundings. All friendships begin with a smile, maybe a handshake, and definitely good conversation. Spring and summer are great times for neighbors to get to know each other. When you find a neighbor out working in her yard you can comment on her flowers, or on the crabgrass growing in your own lawn, or on the beautiful day. You can proceed to tell your neighbor about your morning, and mention and ask about interests, talents, and hobbies.

2. Invite her to do something with you. Friendshipping a non-Mormon neighbor is really not very different than enjoying activities with member friends. Of course, you can't invite her to go to the temple with you on ward temple night, but how about asking your neighbor to walk with you for the exercise? (Many indoor malls are open early in the morning to accommodate veteran walkers during bad weather.) This is a great way to get to know someone in a comfortable setting. If you run out of things to talk about, it's all right. You will probably both be out of breath anyway.

If your neighbor has children, invite her to ride with you to a PTA meeting, or invite the children to come over to meet your children and the mother to stay and visit with you. Offer invitations to family outings, or just to go out to lunch. Have a few friends over to play games and include your neighbor.

Don't be overly concerned with a person's bad habits. The Word of Wisdom does not need to be a line of division between Mormons and everyone else. The burden of Mormons and non-Mormons alike is to be respectful of those who are different. If your friends like a light alcoholic drink with their dinner at the restaurant, they should not be made to feel judged. You can refuse coffee or alcohol politely with a simple "no thank you." "I don't believe in using that stuff" is a put-down and a value judgment to those who see nothing wrong with it. If smoking is annoying but not nauseating to you, offer on occasion to sit in the smoking section of the restaurant.

3. Involve your nonmember and less-active friends and neighbors in activities that center around the Church. We have so many wonderful church programs: pageants, plays, concerts, Tabernacle Choir broadcasts, visitor center tours, Relief Society homemaking night, and don't forget the road show! These can be nonthreatening places where the gospel of Jesus Christ is all around, but not pushed. The exciting thing about getting a neighbor involved with many members of the Church is that she begins to know them and feel comfortable around them. Church no longer seems frightening or uncomfortable because it is a place where friends are found.

4. When your friend or neighbor feels comfortable being inside the church building, invite her to attend church with you. This step is often frightening, because once you have invested so much time and love in a new relationship, you don't want to risk destroying it by offending that person. However, your friends may see it differently; they may think they haven't been invited because they are not wanted or not welcome. An invitation says, "I want you with me." Being turned down can mean anything: "I don't have time." "I don't want to get involved." "I'm frightened of this new experience." "I don't feel like attending that church meeting." Whatever you do, don't take a rejection of an invitation as a personal rejection of you! Your friend can still love you very much, yet not accept the gospel.

Of course, we would like all our friends to join the Church so they can share in the great joy the gospel brings, but friendships should not end because the waters of baptism or the doors to reactivity are not penetrated or opened. You can have a close, loving relationship with those who may not share your habits or beliefs. Those golden friends who are outside your comfortable circle of Mormon companions will add great joy to your life!

Love Encircles Enemies

The Lord has commanded, "Love your enemies, bless them that curse you, do good to them that hate you, and pray for them which despitefully use you, and persecute you." Then he explained why this commandment is so important: "That ye may be the children of your Father which is in heaven." (Matthew 5:44-45.) Our Heavenly Father loves all his children, both the wicked and the righteous, and commands us to do likewise so that we can learn to be as he is.

A mother tells how her children put this principle into practice:

> My two sons were having a lot of trouble with the little boy next door. Whenever they would go out to play, John would sit on the fence and call them names or throw dirt clods at them. This went on week after week. At first, my sons threw the dirt back at him. This just made things worse. My advice to "just ignore him" didn't work. He was chasing them out of their own backyard. I talked to his mother, but still the behavior continued.
>
> Finally, in a family council meeting, we discussed the problem. "How would Jesus handle this situation?" we asked each other. As we looked a little closer at the boy, we realized that he never

played with anyone. Maybe he was lonely and trying to get attention. We decided to befriend him.

A few days later one of my sons came running in the house. "Do you have an extra cookie for John?" he asked. Then almost bubbling over my son explained, "John climbed the fence, but before he threw anything at us, I said, 'Would you like to come and play in the sandpile?' Now he's playing with us."

Our problems with John are not over, but they are certainly a lot better.

When Abraham Lincoln once said a few good-hearted words about the Confederates an irate woman snapped, "How can you say kind things about your enemies? You should want to destroy them!"

Lincoln answered, "What, Madam, do I not destroy them when I make them my friends?"

Sometimes our "enemies" are the flaws and faults in ourselves and in other people. These imperfections often cause conflicts and discord. The Lord pleaded with Peter, "Feed my sheep." His plea goes out to each of us. However, in order to feed the Lord's sheep, we must get right in amongst the flock. When we do, we find that the perfect, docile, little lamb that followed Mary to school is found only in the nursery rhymes. *All* the Lord's sheep have blemishes. Maybe they bleat too loud, or stir up dust, or eat too much of the grass, or don't produce the finest quality wool. We may be tempted to shun others because of their short-comings, but as disciples of Christ we must choose to continue to love. Where there is bitterness and hatred the Holy Spirit cannot dwell.

One sister lived close to her extended family. Heartbreaking experiences descended upon her relatives and, through it all, this sister was always at their side, giving support and caring for their needs. She had endured many insults and backbiting comments from those relatives, and yet always rallied to their aid and defense. Although this sister received no outward rewards expressed in thanks or appreciation, her spiritual rewards were great. She felt at peace knowing that she followed Christ's example.

It can be a blessing rather than a curse to learn that our friends and family are not perfect, because then we might worry less about our own imperfections. Richard L. Evans said, "Perhaps any of us could get along with perfect people. But our task is to get along with imperfect people." As we learn to love unconditionally, perhaps our example will enable others to accept our faults and love us unconditionally in return. Maybe our love will even soften the hearts of those who reject us.

We must be aware, as we feed the Lord's sheep, that we might get snapped at by a wolf carefully disguised in soft sheep's wool. Because of this possibility, we do need to use some caution. In the Book of Mormon, when the Nephites or Lamanites were righteous they prayed for their enemies and even tried to convert them, but they also planned carefully to protect themselves against destruction. There are some people who may purposely seek to take advantage of, abuse, or destroy you or those you love — emotionally, spiritually, financially, or physically. You can love them yet safeguard yourself at the same time.

Consider the following examples:

Case 1: Mary and Joan are neighbors. Joan is very loving and giving. At first, it seems that Mary has much the same personality, but Joan soon notices that Mary is constantly pointing out her faults and criticizing her. At first these little jabs are conducted in the name of friendship: "I just want you to know for your own good what people are saying behind your back." But soon the back stabs deteriorate into frontal attacks: sometimes in private, sometimes in public, sometimes camouflaged as jests and jokes. The negative abuse begins to undermine Joan's feelings of self-worth.

Your task is to love, yet you must also be cautious about people who wish to demean and demolish you. Those who love you will want to help you be a better person. But there is certainly an appropriate way to give constructive criticism. The Lord teaches such a way in his counsel on righteous exercise of priesthood authority—a method that applies well to all relationships. He says, "Reproving betimes with sharpness, when moved upon by the Holy Ghost; and then showing forth afterwards an increase of love toward him whom thou hast reproved, lest he esteem thee to be his enemy." (D&C 121:43.)

The second word in this scriptural reference is *betimes*. It is sometimes mistakenly interpreted as *sometimes* or *many times,* but actually it is an archaic word meaning *early* or *before it is too late.* A person who loves you will let you know that you are on the wrong path before you have gone too far to turn around, but by her words and actions you will know that her "faithfulness is stronger than the cords of death." (D&C 121:44.)

There is a vast difference between being lovingly criticized and unjustly put down. The first is like a gift of love brought to the door of your soul; the second is like a planted bomb, that, if allowed to detonate, will leave the spirit filled with shrapnel of self-doubt, self-distrust, even self-contempt.

> Case 2: Margaret and Jeanne have been next-door neighbors for years. Margaret suddenly shows an interest in the Church, borrowing church books and other literature from Jeanne, which causes great excitement in Jeanne's family. Jeanne takes Margaret to church and introduces the missionaries to her. At first everything seems to go smoothly. Then Margaret begins to challenge the missionaries, using a belligerent tone. She points out the faults of all her Mormon neighbors and finally pulls out anti-Mormon literature and shoves it at the missionaries and Jeanne. Communication completely breaks down when Margaret argues with anything Jeanne and the missionaries say. Because some of the things Margaret quotes seem logical and because Jeanne doesn't have all the answers, she becomes confused and begins to doubt her testimony.

You must continue to love, yet realize that people who find it amusing to take potshots at sacred things may eventually mortally wound your spirit. There are a few people, sometimes members in good standing, who habitually criticize the organizations, leaders, and even doctrines of the Church. Continuing a close relationship with such people is like sitting in a room where someone is smoking: even though you may not be contributing to the air pollution, some of the rank odor is sure to cling to you.

There are other times when it is wise to turn your back on a relationship and quickly walk far away. Elder Boyd K. Packer mentions two such situations:

"If someone approaches you individually or invites you to very private meetings, claiming to have some special calling, whatever you do, follow Paul's counsel—'from such turn away.'

". . . . There are some who, motivated by one influence or another, seek through writing and publishing criticisms and interpretations of doctrine to make the gospel more acceptable to the so-called thinking people of the world. . . . If their spirits are pure and their motives worthy, they will do no harm either to themselves or to others. If they are not, we would all do well to follow Paul's admonition and 'from such turn away.'" (Taken from the *Ensign*, May 1985, p. 35.)

Case 3: A long lost mission companion, let's call him Mark, called John one day. "Hey, buddy, I would just love to see you. It's been ten years, hasn't it?"

John was a bit confused by this sudden interruption from his past, but he was also flattered to be remembered, so he invited Mark to his home to meet his wife.

The appointed day arrived and so did Mark. After several minutes of chitchat Mark got right down to business. "How would you and your wife like to never have any financial problems again?" He launched into a sales pitch for a pyramid

scheme. "Right now you can get in on the ground
level . . . just have to sell it to your friends . . . get
them to join . . . be doing them a favor . . . easy
money."

John is a quiet and polite man. He listened,
then, trying to keep the anger from his voice, he
invited his "friend" to leave.

The Mormon people have often been targeted by criminals
as easy marks. Because we are taught to be honest and trustworthy,
we often assume — sometimes too readily — that everyone else has
accepted the same teachings. It is always an unhappy surprise
when one of our own brothers or sisters in the Church is accused
or convicted of a crime. We learn over and over again that out
of the best nesting grounds hatch some very bad eggs. We also
learn that Satan is happy to incubate and import as many rotten
eggs as he can find. We must love even these, yet we need to
stay far way from their schemes.

Case 4: Sometimes financial abuse of a friendship is very closely linked to physical or substance
abuse. Bill, a known pusher, tried to deliver drugs
to a young woman who had sworn to go straight.
As subtle and devious as the serpent in the Garden
of Eden, Bill tried every device he could think of to
get the young woman to partake of the forbidden
fruit, but she refused. "Okay, but when you want it,
don't go to a stranger." He pointed to himself and
added, "Remember to call your friend."

A friend will not seek to destroy your life to put dollars in
his pocket; in doing so he has sold his friendship. This is a
common type of betrayal in our history. We read in the Bible
of Judas, one of the twelve, a chosen friend in the Savior's closest
circle, betraying the Christ for thirty pieces of silver. The scriptural account is revealing:

"And while he yet spake, lo, Judas, one of the twelve, came, and with him a great multitude with swords and staves, from the chief priests and elders of the people.

"Now he that betrayed him gave them a sign, saying, Whomsoever I shall kiss, that same is he: hold him fast.

"And forthwith he came to Jesus, and said, Hail, master; and kissed him.

"And Jesus said unto him, *Friend*, wherefore art thou come? Then came they, and laid hands on Jesus, and took him." (Matthew 26:47-50; italics added.)

Can you feel the sadness in our Savior's voice because of the betrayal of one he called "friend"? Yet the Lord continued to love even Judas.

No matter what the circumstance may be, we must continue to love. But as long as a person's words or actions remain damaging to you, keep her at a distance and proceed with the relationship only under inspiration. Never be rude or bitter. You can be loving and kind, yet not allow that person into your inner circle where she can tear up or pull down that which you have worked so hard to build.

The Lord states definitely that we should be willing to forgive anyone who harms us. "For, if ye forgive men their trespasses your heavenly Father will also forgive you." (3 Nephi 13:14.) And we should always allow for repentance and a changed heart. "Come now, and let us reason together, saith the Lord: though your sins be as scarlet, they shall be as white as snow; though they be red like crimson, they shall be as wool." (Isaiah 1:18.) Our Heavenly Father has given us almost unlimited space to turn around and come back. We, the children of our Heavenly Father, can do no less for our brothers and sisters.

CHAPTER 10

Love Encircles Distances

As our feelings of charity grow, we eventually come to the realization that we need to include everyone in our circle of love. As the years pass, we have opportunities to meet a multitude of people. They move in and out of our neighborhoods and wards. Sometimes we are the ones that must leave and make a new home. It is difficult to meet all these people, and impossible to develop and maintain a loving relationship with each one. Because of this obstacle, many people don't try to meet anyone new. Some people even feel that if you can't make a lasting friendship, there is no need to get acquainted or introduce yourself at all. For these reasons, people living in apartments or renting homes, or those who are only visiting and attending church meetings for a day, are sometimes ignored.

A sister from Hawaii who visited a ward in Salt Lake City observed, "It sure is different here. When you attend church in Hawaii, no matter who you are, everyone comes up to greet you and give you a big aloha hug. Here, no one even asked who I was until after all the meetings were over."

Sometimes people who know that they must move again refuse to get involved with their neighbors and ward. "I just don't want to get too close," one sister admitted, "because I know I won't be staying here long and it will make me sadder if I have to leave friends behind."

Thus, we miss many opportunities for adding joy to our own

lives or those of others. What a shame! It doesn't need to be this way. These barriers to unconditional love can be removed if we will just be willing to look beyond the distances and view eternity. There are several steps we can take to enlarge our limited perspective:

1. We need to remind ourselves that we will not always have such severe time restrictions. A sister who was planning to move out of her ward soon continued to make it a point to meet all the new people moving in. "I know that I don't have the time to really get to know them now, but there will be plenty of time later on in the eternities," she said. "By beginning the friendship here, I will just be that much further ahead in the hereafter."

2. We need to recognize that there are many different types of relationships and all of them are important. Friendships are like flowers. Some bud briefly and then they are gone. Still others blossom, but only for a season. Then there are special varieties that grow, bursting out in brilliant colors, year after year. Just as people who love flowers include all varieties in their gardens, we who seek to reach out and love as Jesus did need to include all types of relationships in our lives. Some who are not overly ambitious gardeners are always seeking the ever-blossoming flower that only has to be planted once and then can be largely ignored after that. In your search for that perfect friendship, don't miss all the others, no matter how brief their blooming season.

3. We need to be more concerned about what we can add to another person's life and less concerned about what that person will add to or take away from our life. Hollie was planning a move to a new city. As the construction work was being completed on her new home, she was released from her church callings. During the final visiting teaching interview with her Relief Society president, Hollie was prompted to ask, "Is there anyone in the ward who especially needs to be loved? Who needs me?"

Looking troubled, the Relief Society president said, "I can't believe you asked that! There is someone. I've been praying for answer on how to reach her. She has requested not to have visiting teachers anymore." Hollie learned that this sister was someone she knew, loved, and had worked with over the years in ward and stake callings:

I invited my friend to lunch, which was not a common, everyday thing, but something rather out of the ordinary. I'm sure it was mostly out of curiosity that my friend accepted my invitation, however, nothing was voiced about the unusual lunch outing until we were seated in the restaurant and prepared to order from the menu.

"Well, do you want to know why I invited you to lunch?" I asked with a silent prayer in my heart.

"Of course," she cautiously nodded. "What's up?"

Not ever being one to beat around the bush, I went right to the point, "I've been asked to be your visiting teacher, and I'm praying that you won't turn me down."

Time stopped. It was as if the world around us became a motionless void of background scenery. She focused directly at my eyes, neither of us moving, until I saw the tears swelling across her unblinking lids and steadily increasing until they burst like a waterfall down her cheek.

"I don't want a visiting teacher," she quietly and distinctly said. "I just can't have one." Each word was uttered with obvious strained control.

"I know that you don't want one, but Heavenly Father said, 'No.' It is not his plan or intention that you should *not* have a visiting teacher."

"But, you don't understand," she said with anguish in her voice.

I interrupted her worry and assured her, "I *do* understand. I don't know what's happened, but I *do know* that you have a great hurt within you, and *that* I understand. Please let me be your friend and visiting teacher! Please, please don't shut me out too."

Our hands, which were across the table from each other, pushed forward to touch. We continued looking at each other; both our eyes were filled with tears from sharing the unspoken words of our feelings and emotions. Her head slowly bowed as she whispered her acceptance to my offer.

In the last weeks before Hollie moved she succeeded in being an instrument in the Lord's hands to give strength to her friend. After Hollie moved, new visiting teachers were called and they were once again welcome in her friend's home. Although she left her neighborhood, Hollie didn't leave this friend to struggle alone. Because of the special feelings of tenderness these two friends felt toward each other, they have persisted in their commitment of friendship even though distances separated them.

4. We need to realize that distances need not dim relationships. Your friendships can remain as bright as you will allow them to be. Among all the people you meet, there will be a few who continue to pluck at your heartstrings. Just because your paths separate, this does not mean that the calming harmony of the relationship must fade out and die.

Lauren tells about a friendship she has nurtured since childhood:

"Come on, Annie. Please answer the phone," I pleaded in my thoughts. "I really need to talk to you."

I waited as the phone rang several more times. No answer. This was the third time in the space of a week that I had dialed the Washington, D.C., number. As I hung up the phone I began recalling the many experiences that Annie and I had had during the past twenty-one years.

Annie and I met when we were four years old. She lived just one block away from me. For the next four years we were inseparable. We walked to school together, played together, and were constantly sleeping over at each other's houses. Annie was my best friend.

The summer before we entered third grade, Annie and her family moved across town. Both of us were heartbroken. We wouldn't even be going to the same school together anymore. Still our friendship endured. Going to movies together and the "sleeping over" practice continued as often as our parents would allow. The autumn we began junior high was wonderful. We were together at last in the same school. Suffering through the same algebra course, tolerating the same creepy boys, and nearly driving our home economics teacher crazy with our giggling, our friendship blossomed and deepened. We sang together, walked together, cried together, and talked together. Years passed and we entered high school. That first year is filled with memories of driver's education, girls' chorus, double dates, and the day my parents informed me we were moving to another city. I recalled the flood of tears as Annie and I said goodbye and secretly wondered if our friendship could last over this new and greater distance. We managed to still get together occasionally for double dates and birthdays and we kept each other informed on new boyfriend prospects. After graduating from high school, we attended the same university. Later, when Annie went to France for six months and I went to Alaska to work, we wrote letters. Her letters would be humorously addressed to "Bush Baby Lauren."

Six months later Annie served as my maid of honor when I got married. After Annie married, she left with her husband for Washington, D.C., where he would be attending medical school. Later that year I received the special phone call I had been waiting for. "It's a girl," Annie exclaimed joyfully.

Listening, loving, and caring, Annie had always been there to share the good times and support me through the bad times. Oh, how I needed to talk to her now! "I'll try calling her again later," I promised myself.

Saturday morning I was awakened by the phone ringing. "It's Annie from Washington, D.C.," Bret announced. I immediately wondered if something was wrong. We hadn't talked for several months. Why on earth would she be calling?

I grabbed the phone. Annie greeted me in her usual cheerful voice and I could tell immediately that all was well. Then my emotional dam burst and all of the troubles and worries that had backed up came flooding out. As usual, Annie listened intently and helped me deal with my concerns.

"Annie, I don't know why you called this morning, but I'm sure glad you did," I told her with tears rolling down my cheeks.

"I've just had 'Lauren on the brain' for the past two days and felt that I should call you," she replied.

I don't know what directions each of our lives will take us in the coming years, but I do know that it will never matter how many miles separate us, Annie and I will always be close friends.

When a friend or family member moves away, get a phone number and address as soon as possible. Don't write this vital information on the back of an old envelope or other scrap paper. Record it in your address book immediately. If you have lost the address of a friend, check with your local library. Many libraries keep current phone books from all over the United States.

Continue to remember birthdays and other special holidays. Lisa and Becky bonded a strong friendship while living next door to each other; then Becky moved two hundred miles away. Since their birthdays are within a few days of each other, they decided to meet and have a celebration luncheon in a small town halfway between their two cities. This has become a yearly tradition that has helped them continue a beautiful friendship.

Sending Christmas cards is a great tradition that seems to be dying out. If you have to shorten your list, take off those people to whom you can wish a personal "Merry Christmas," but leave on those who are far away. It is nice to receive a card, to keep in touch, even it is only once a year.

One mother likes to share recipes, cartoons, and newspaper articles with her children who live far away. When time is short she just clips the item, writes "love, Mom" in a corner, and sends it in the mail. Some families have family newsletters. The editor can be changed with each edition, or appointed for a year or more. Everyone in the family contributes by writing personal news flashes.

Some communications get tied down over whose turn it is to write or call. "Well, I called her last time. It's her turn to call me." "I'm not going to write a letter. She didn't answer my last letter." Don't worry about it. Call or write whenever that distant person drifts across your mind.

5. We need to remember that often the Lord answers prayers through our brothers and sisters here on earth. There will still be times, even when miles separate you, that you will be needed or you will need your friends. When that friend calls out for help, or when the Spirit says "Go," then be prepared to answer and obey.

Hollie tells how a spiritually sensitive friend lifted her from despair one New Year's Eve. A letter from Hollie's fiance, calling off their wedding, had left her shattered and empty. The pain from his rejection was swelling inside her this particular night until she thought she would burst. She relates:

> I prayed fervently for help. Didn't someone love me? Didn't someone care?
>
> Then the doorbell rang. *Who rings doorbells at 11:30 P.M.?* I thought. I called out, "Who's there?"
>
> The answer came, "It's Cara."

"Cara!" I shouted and excitedly unlatched the separate locks and threw open the door.

"Cara, what are you doing here?" Cara lived a hundred miles away and was standing on my doorstep with her P.J.'s over one arm and holding a half gallon of ice cream with her other hand.

She looked at me, and ever so sweetly spoke, "I just thought you needed me, so I got in the car and drove straight to your house."

We hugged, and tears fell from the joy of understanding each other. God had heard my prayers, and when I had reached my darkest hour, he had sent an angel to comfort me, a friend—my friend!

During Jesus' time on earth he reached out in love to everyone. Distance wasn't a barrier. His love encircled all those who lived on earth and those who had passed on. His love encircled worlds without number that he had created. His love encircled you, me, and millions of our brothers and sisters who dwelt in a kingdom far away, anxiously awaiting their time to come to earth. We too can reach out and encircle others with love, whether we know them only for a moment or for a lifetime.